Dream With Me

A Dreamer's Ramblings on Life, Love, God, and Achieving the Dream

Books by R.S. Veira

Turner Street: Where the Monsters in the Closet are Real

Turner Street: The Cain Seed

Turner Street: Anomalies

The Last Guardians (Tales of Aela Book One)

Dream With Me

A Dreamer's Ramblings on Life, Love,
God, and Achieving the Dream

R.S. Veira

RSV Ink
An Imprint of Dream With Me Productions

Dream With Me

RSV Ink Edition 2021

Copyright © 2021 R.S. Veira

Published by RSV Ink
Los Angeles, California

Cover design by Laurie Wright
https://www.fiverr.com/lauria

Edited by Vince Font (Glass Spider Publishing)
https://www.glassspiderpublishing.com

All rights reserved. This book or any portion thereof may not be reproduced or used in any manner whatsoever without the express written permission of the publisher except in the case of brief quotations embodied in critical articles and reviews.

RSV Ink books may be purchased for educational, business, or sales promotional use. For information please e-mail RSV Ink at RSVInkbooks@dwmprod.com

Dream With Me Productions Website: https://www.dwmprod.com

Scriptures taken from the Holy Bible, New International Version®, NIV®. Copyright © 1973, 1978, 1984, 2011 by Biblica, Inc.™ Used by permission of Zondervan. All rights reserved worldwide. www.zondervan.com The "NIV" and "New International Version" are trademarks registered in the United States Patent and Trademark Office by Biblica, Inc.™

This book is comprised of the author's memories and personal experiences. Some names have been omitted, some events have been compressed, and some dialogue has been recreated. This is his story as he remembers it.

FIRST RSV INK PAPERBACK EDITION PUBLISHED IN 2021

Library of Congress Control Number: 2021911817

ISBN 978-1-7369742-8-5

EPUB ISBN 978-1-7369742-9-2

For Larry, Gabrielle, Zach & the Dreamers

Table of Contents

Foreword	I
Preface	V
The Origin of a Dreamer	IX
Dream With Me	1
A Sit-Down With a Dreamer: Laurie Lazzaro Knowlton	6
Keep Calm & Enjoy the Journey	11
How Will You Be Remembered?	14
Success is No Accident	18
Ramblings on Life – February 19th, 2014 – 7:18AM	23
Why We Must Embrace the Little Things	25
Finding Self-Motivation	29
There's More to Being a Dreamer than Dreaming	33
Faith	37
Doubt	41
Ramblings on Life – October 15th, 2014 – 11:00PM	45
A Sit-Down With a Dreamer: Rich Morrow	47
How to Beat a Slump	53
What I Learned in Third Grade	57

Watch the Company You Keep	61
Season Finale	65
Ramblings on Love – November 21st, 2016 – 2:39AM	71
Passion, Where Art Thou?	73
A Sit-Down With a Dreamer: Antonio Veira	77
We Could All Use a Break	82
Run Your Race	86
200%	90
Ramblings on Love – July 25th, 2014 – 1:09AM	95
Grind in Silence	97
Seize the Day	100
Decisions, Decisions	103
Learning from the Greats	107
Ramblings on Life – November 20th, 2016 – 10:32PM	111
Keep Calm & Enjoy the Journey 2	113
Is the Juice Worth the Squeeze?	117
What a Time to Chase a Dream	120
Crunch Time	124
Here & Now	128
Ramblings on God – August 22nd, 2020 – 3:03AM	133

The Person in the Mirror	137
Learning from the Greats 2	141
2015: A Year in Review	146
A Day of Thanks	150
Blueprint for Success	154
Ramblings on God – November 23rd, 2020 – 11:57PM	159
A Good Poker Face	161
Do You	165
Rerouting…	169
Who's Listening?	173
No Worries	176
Ramblings on Love – August 14th, 2019 – 3:06AM	181
Keep Calm & Enjoy the Journey 3	185
Mamba Out	189
Enjoying the View	192
Keep Calm & Enjoy the Journey 4	196
In Due Time	200
Ramblings on Life – January 18th, 2020 – 6:55PM	205
A Satisfying Ending	207
Balancing Expectations	211

Keep Calm & Enjoy the Journey 5	215
Blessings at Hand	219
Ramblings on Life – February 18th, 2020 – 5:04AM	223
Definiteness of Purpose	225
Calm Satisfaction	229
Keep Calm & Enjoy the Journey 6	233
The Matrix of Miracles	236
My 4-Year To-Do List (2014-2018)	240
Ramblings on Life – November 18th, 2019 – 2:58AM	245
Managing Disappointment	247
From the Ashes I Rose	251
Two Sides of the Same Coin	254
Ramblings on Love – August 17th, 2019 – 4:50AM	259
A Decade of Highs & Sighs	261
Why Do We Do What We Do?	265
The Shattering of My Fetters	269
Ramblings on God – February 23rd, 2021 – 2:14AM	275
Submission (A Poem)	279
About the Author	281

"Happy are those who dream dreams and are ready to pay the price to make them come true."

— Leon Joseph Suenens

Foreword

by

Laurie Lazzaro Knowlton

As the author of more than 40 books in the trade—Christian, educational, craft, and work-for-hire markets—I was asked to speak at the Medina County Library in Medina, Ohio. My speech addressed the process of self-editing manuscripts for submission to publishers. The majority of the crowd was made up of middle-aged and older dreamers who desperately wanted to crack the code of getting their work published.

Afterwards, I was surrounded by people asking questions. One young man waited patiently. He introduced himself as Raphael Veira, a senior college student. He had a book query and asked if I would take a look. Over the next few months, we e-mailed, talked by phone, and met. Each time we spoke, I was impressed by this young man's consistent dream of publication. Raphael was dedicated to learning the craft of writing. He understood the importance of building a brand and developing an internet presence. He believed in his God-given talents. He was articulate and mature beyond his age and a joy to mentor.

Once when we talked, he asked what I thought about his desire to pursue screenwriting in Los Angeles. I encouraged him to follow his desire because I knew Raphael had a good sense of who he was and what his goals were. We discussed family, his faith, his dream goal of achieving publication, and the changes he would experience by moving to the West Coast.

When we spoke, I expressed my thoughts on true success. I believe success comes through the following actions:

1.) **God:** You need to have a working and personal relationship with our heavenly Father.

2.) **Tenacity:** Writing is not for the faint of heart. You have to be able to take rejection and keep on working, perfecting your craft.

3.) **Talent:** Everyone has God-given talents. But it is your job to hone your skills.

4.) **Timing:** For everything there is a season. For me, it took 12 years of rejections while I watched friends I'd helped get published…It wasn't my time *YET.*

5.) **Sharing:** This journey of writing is a well-beaten path of people ahead of you and people behind you. Others have reached back to help you. Now it is time for you to share your knowledge and help others.

Since Raphael moved to Los Angeles, I have watched him grow in his relationship with God. I've read of his tenacity in the face of disappointments. He's constantly worked at developing his talent and has been patiently waiting for God's timing. Through his writing, he has been willing to share his passion, his failures, and his successes, while encouraging his following.

Foreword

Raphael's heartfelt blogs are a reflection of his ongoing dreams. Readers of *Dream With Me* will experience Raphael's sincere, hope-filled, helpful writing journey and be changed by the honesty and depths of this awesome collection of blogs.

Preface

Dream *With Me: A Dreamer's Ramblings on Life, Love, God, and Achieving the Dream* is comprised of a collection of blog posts and personal notes I wrote between 2014-2021. In its pages, you'll witness not only a dream come to fruition, but a young man stepping into manhood. You'll experience the ups and downs of my journey from Cleveland to Los Angeles to become an author, writer, and director. You'll see the birth of my production company, Dream With Me Productions LLC, and my imprint, RSV Ink, which published this book. Most importantly, however, you'll see God's faithfulness and the awesomeness of His work.

Between every five or so blog posts is a personal note titled "Ramblings on" either Life, Love, or God. These are notes I wrote to myself that provide a glimpse into my thoughts at the time. As you'll see, each blog post and note is dated. In editing this book, I tried my best to preserve the heart of the original writing of each note and blog post while also providing touch-ups and minor additions where necessary.

I decided to present the blog posts as they originally appeared on my website, including the titles and structure. Also, not every blog post I wrote made it into this collection. My aim was to not

Preface

only inspire but to create a narrative arc—and hopefully not repeat myself too much. With that being said, I also believe you can pick up this book at any time, turn to any blog post or note, and enjoy what you read.

I started my blog in 2015 with the hope of not only building my audience as an author, but to hopefully provide inspiration to anyone who was willing to throw caution to the wind, walk by faith, and chase their dreams. I release this book into the world praying that it does the same.

If you're reading this, I'm grateful and thankful that this book found you. I pray that it inspires you to not only dream without constraint but to give all you have to your dream's fulfillment, no matter the lengths. I promise you, if you do, you will not be disappointed by your choice. In this book, I humbly share with you a part of my soul in the hope that it ignites a fire in yours.

Now, I must thank everyone who is mentioned (and not mentioned) in this book for all the support you have given to me and my dreams over the years. In particular, I would like to take this time to thank my friends, teachers, and coaches from both University School (US) and John Hay; all my basketball teammates from AAU, US, John Hay, and Cleveland State University (CSU); my friends from Xavier University; the amazing basketball coaching staff at CSU led by Gary Waters; and finally all my friends and mentors in both Cleveland and Los Angeles who filled me with the knowledge and confidence to pursue writing and directing. I would be remiss if I did not mention my best friend, business partner, and brother, Landen Amos. He too ventured out to LA with a dream and has been nothing but a steadfast friend.

A special thanks must now be given to my aunts, uncles, cous-

Preface

ins, and godparents who showered me with love in my youth and continue to be my staunchest supporters.

At last, and certainly not least, I come to my immediate family, who I thank God for every single day. My brother, Antonio, and my sisters, Danielle and Gabrielle, who continually inspire me with the depth of their love and the strength of their character. Finally, thank you to my parents, Diana Eldemire Veira and Anthony St. Michael Veira, for loving me, guiding me, defending me, and instilling in me a true love of life and of God.

The Origin of a Dreamer

My name is Raphael Sylvester Veira, aka R.S. Veira, and I am the son of dreamers.

My father, Anthony St. Michael Veira, was born in 1959 to Cynthia Johnston and Sydney Veira. He was raised by his mother, Cynthia, in Kingston, Jamaica. As a boy, he walked the majestic island's rough streets dreaming of better days. In particular, he dreamed of building his own business and constructing a home similar to those of the affluent, which dotted the suburban hillside of Kingston. He dreamed and prayed that he could do all this with a strong, beautiful, and intelligent Jamaican woman. In the deepest parts of his heart, he hoped that God would also bless them with a family so that he could be the father to them that he never had.

When Anthony was about 14, he immigrated to the United States to live with his mother. She had left him in the care of his great-grandmother when he was a boy while she paved a way for him to join her in the States. Over the next 40 years, my father steadily, with the help of the Almighty, breathed life into the dreams he had as a child. He went to Shaw High School, then Ohio State University, and ultimately graduated from Cleveland

State University. Along the way, he met and married Diana Eldemire Veira, a strong, beautiful, intelligent Jamaican woman.

In the late '80s, he founded Computer Connectivity Incorporated (CCI), a computer consulting firm, and then in the '90s he dove into real estate and co-founded Touchstone Management Ltd., a real estate investment and management company, with his wife, Diana. During this time, he also started a family and built his dream home in Cleveland, Ohio. He was and is an upright, steadfast, and amazing father to his children: Antonio, Danielle, Raphael, and Gabrielle. He's a dreamer who fulfilled and is living out his dream.

My mother, Diana Eldemire Veira, was born in 1957 in Cleveland, Ohio. She's the daughter of Gauntlett Sylvester Eldemire I and Minerva Jeanetta Gardner, both of whom emigrated from Jamaica. When she was nine years old, her mother tragically passed due to a brain aneurysm, and Diana was thrust into the role of caretaker. While her father labored to create an inheritance for his four children, which he ultimately accomplished in the form of the real estate properties he acquired and maintained, Diana was tasked with watching over her younger siblings.

Gauntlett Sylvester Eldemire I, her father, was an illegitimate son born to a family with a rich history in Jamaican politics, healthcare, and real estate. He fled to the United States to escape the stigma of illegitimacy and to begin a new life with Minerva. After his wife's death, he threw himself deeper into his dream of creating a substantial real estate portfolio for his children to inherit. This did not go unnoticed by my mother. Inspired, Diana dreamed of one day building her own real estate company. She dreamed and prayed that she would build this company with a man who truly loved her in mind, body, and soul, and who would recognize the rich Jamaican heritage of the Eldemire name.

On her journey to realize her dream, she went to Shaw High School, then Wilberforce University, and ultimately graduated from Cleveland State University. Diana went from managing editor of the Vindicator, CSU's Black newspaper, to computer programmer at General Electric, and then to Director of Data Services at Ameritech. During all of this, she met and married Anthony St. Michael Veira, a handsome and determined Jamaican man who not only loved her completely but recognized the deep Jamaican roots of her last name. Together, they founded and built Touchstone Management Ltd. She gave birth to three children: Danielle, Raphael, and Gabrielle Veira. She was and is a devoted, nurturing, and inspiring mother. She is a dreamer who fulfilled and is living out her dream.

These two dreamers brought me into the world, and I am forever thankful to my parents for instilling in me the belief that my dreams can be my reality.

I've always believed that in order to live a fully realized life, one must first find their passion, pursue it with unrelenting determination and unwavering focus, and then do their best to do everything out of love. This was made all the more real to me by watching how my parents lived their lives and how they selflessly supported my dreams.

I was blessed to discover my passions early on: writing, basketball, and inspiring others. All three of these directly led to the creation of this book. The fulfillment of my hoop dreams instilled in me the needed confidence in myself—and, more importantly, in God—to pursue my writing ambitions. Along the way, I tried my best to inspire others to chase their dreams by sharing bits of my journey. My journey to become the author, director, and dreamer that I am today is for the most part told in these pages, but the foundation that made all that possible was laid during my pursuit to fulfill my hoop dreams. I believe for you to truly understand and appreciate the latter, you first must know the former.

I love basketball. It's a game that immediately captured my heart and imagination. I dreamed of playing at the highest level I could, and all my thoughts and actions were in line with that dream. As a teenager, many of my days were spent hooping; it didn't matter if it was indoors, outdoors, rain, snow, or shine. The concrete court and hoop my father built in our backyard was my sanctuary. I was in love, and I gave my heart to the game. However, as anyone with a dream knows, it wasn't long before the haters and the obstacles made themselves known.

From kindergarten to 11th grade, I attended University School (US), a top-flight all-boys prep school in Cleveland, Ohio. I have amazing memories from my time at US, and I forged lifelong friendships in the fires of its rigorous academic curriculum. Yet it was in these same halls where I faced the first true obstruction to the fulfillment of my dream.

I decided to transfer during my senior year of high school because of the unjust treatment I believed I was receiving on the basketball court. I knew I had the ability to play. I had been on the varsity team in some capacity since my sophomore year. I believed I had shown the necessary commitment to the team. I was a staple at morning workouts and regularly stayed late to put up extra shots, but my coach rarely found time for me. This begat not only a testy relationship between us, but it fostered in me a deep resentment toward him. I believed that he was standing directly in the way of my dream and was personally holding me down from soaring. However, few understood my angst. They reasoned that if I was truly as good as I believed, I would be playing—which I understood, to an extent. Nevertheless, I was at a crossroads. Either transfer, bet on myself and the dream God planted in my soul, or let my dream die. I decided to transfer.

This decision, however, was not an easy one. At the end of my junior year, I had been elected as one of the 10 US house prefects. At US, the entire student body was divided into 10 houses. Each was named after either a founder of the school, previous headmaster, or influential member of the school's community. The houses compete throughout the year in order to win the coveted House Cup, which was awarded at the end of the year. US was also split into two campuses. A lower school for grades K-8 in Shaker Heights, and an upper school in Hunting Valley. At the lower school, the houses were led by eighth-grade house captains, and at the upper school by the house prefects. I had been my house's eighth-grade captain, and I always dreamed of being prefect. I had fulfilled that dream, and it killed me to have to walk away from it. It also pained me that I would not graduate with my friends, many of whom I'd known since kindergarten.

Still, all of that was trivial compared to mustering up the courage needed to tell my parents, who had invested greatly in my education, that I could not graduate from US and had to transfer somewhere else in order to pursue my dream. To my parents' credit, they supported me, even if at first it was understandably begrudgingly. It has to be noted that I had not played meaningful varsity minutes to that point in my career. Yet there I was, telling them I needed to transfer in my senior year in order to find a place where I could play basketball because I felt God was telling me I had to. Thankfully, as dreamers themselves, they understood the importance of following a dream.

Everything that happened next I attribute to the gracious hand of God. I've learned in my life that once you decide to go after a dream, God will supply the means, and this was exactly what He did. Once my parents were on board and the decision was final, I soon learned of John Hay and met Coach Sanders.

John Hay High School is a Cleveland public school that opened in 1929 but had closed down in the early 2000s. However, by the '06-'07 school year, it had fully reopened after undergoing remodeling. It reopened as three different schools under the John Hay umbrella: Cleveland Early College High School, Cleveland School of Science and Medicine, and Cleveland School of Architecture & Design. The combination of their rising academic standards and a fantastic pitch from Mr. Weber, the principal of the School of Science and Medicine, and Coach Sanders helped to appease my parents' concerns. Coach Sanders appeased mine.

Coach Sanders' genuine belief in my ability was all I needed to make the move. He wanted to rebuild the basketball program, and I was more than willing to help. He took a chance on a kid with a dream, and I'm forever thankful for that. I enrolled at John Hay's Cleveland School of Science and Medicine and joined the Class of 2010, the first graduating class since its reopening. I had gone from an all-boys private school to a co-ed public school. I was in a whole different world.

I wish I could tell you that it was smooth sailing from there, but that was not the case. As it usually goes on the journey to fulfill our dreams, as I drew closer to the dream's realization, I was met with even more adversity. After transferring, I was soon ruled ineligible by the Ohio High School Athletic Association

(OHSAA). Interestingly enough, there had been a number of other students who had also transferred into John Hay that same year, but I was the only one singled out.

In order to be eligible, I was told I had to live in the school district in which I was transferring. So my father and I moved in with my now-late great-uncle. We settled in with him in his two-bedroom apartment in Cleveland in a building owned by Touchstone Management Ltd., my parents' real estate company. However, I was still ruled ineligible, and by this time, the basketball season had begun. Things were not looking good. I had transferred schools, left all I knew, and I still wasn't playing. Thankfully, my parents decided to take the matter to court. God then raised up a team of lawyers, spearheaded by my aunt, who took up my case pro bono. They managed to get an injunction that allowed me to play two games while they continued to work the matter out.

My first two varsity basketball games at John Hay were lackluster. I scored **14 points over two games.** I underperformed and was thoroughly embarrassed with myself. The morning after the second game, I found myself at the courthouse, waiting to hear the final decision on my remaining eligibility. I'll never forget that day. I sat dejected in the courthouse, wallowing in self-pity and failure. I reflected on my journey to that point. I had talked a big game, transferred high schools, and caused my parents to sleep under separate roofs. On top of that, a team of lawyers had valiantly fought and temporarily won my freedom. Yet, when it was time to perform, I repaid them and myself with **14 points over two games.** It was tragic. As my hands somberly cradled my head, my eyes caught a glimpse of a discarded newspaper at my feet. It happened to be turned to the box scores in the Sports section.

I saw the John Hay box score from the night before, and the ***four points*** I had scored next to my name. It was then I turned to God and prayed. I prayed that if He gave me another shot, I would not be scared. I would do what I knew I could do with the ability He gave me. I concluded my prayer by promising to always talk of His faithfulness if He did so. It was then that my aunt triumphantly emerged from the courtroom and informed my parents and me that I would be eligible for the remainder of the season. We had a game that night, and I was playing.

That night, we played John F. Kennedy High School, which was a top-25 team in the area. We won, and I had 25 points and 12 rebounds. We went on an eight-game winning streak. A few newspaper articles were written that highlighted the turnaround happening at John Hay, and I was named Plain Dealer Player of the Week. At the end of the year, I won team MVP and was a City All-Star. I even got some attention from a few Division I colleges who were interested in having me walk-on. It was a glorious time. I felt vindicated and vowed to always follow my dreams from then on, no matter how great the obstacles or vitriolic the naysayers.

After my senior year at John Hay, I spent a year and a half at Xavier University, where I did not play, before transferring to Cleveland State University. It was there where I walked-on to the basketball team and eventually graduated. During those two years at CSU, basketball took me around the country and the world. My teammates and coaches became family, and at the end of my senior year I won the Horizon League Sportsmanship Award. I look back at this time with nothing but love and appreciation. It was through this journey to fulfill my hoop dreams that God proved to me that He's faithful, and it was how that journey ended that showed me He's truly loving.

Following my senior year at CSU, I hung up my basketball shoes and began to seriously consider pursuing a career as a novelist. During this time, I found myself at a random CSU game. I came to support my former teammates and in some ways to officially say goodbye to my playing days. During halftime, I was unexpectedly approached by my former basketball coach from US. I was standing at the concession stand when he tapped me on the shoulder. I turned around, and at first I wasn't sure how to react. This was someone who I believed had done me a great injustice and who I resented for it; but at the same time, his doubt had pushed me to achieve my dream of playing at the highest level I could. In light of the latter, I was willing to hear what he had to say, and what he said surprised me.

He told me, "Raph, I'm glad you never let anyone stop you from achieving your dream."

I smiled and thanked him. Truthfully, I had no idea how much I needed to hear that from him until I did. All of my resentment dissipated, and I was able to forgive. With that, my basketball dream officially came to a close, and I was at peace with that journey. The foundation had been laid, and I knew if God was with me, I could do anything. The journey may be trying and heart-wrenching at times, but in the end, it all works out. I then officially set my heart, mind, and soul on my new dream to be an author.

It's the journey I went on to achieve this new dream that I wish to share with you in this book. So without further ado, come dream with me…

Dream With Me

January 16th, 2015

Since I was a big-headed boy, I've had a problem accepting the world the way it presented itself to me. The world, or our society, claims to value innovative and out-of-the-box thinking, but its practices don't support such claims.

For example, those of us who try to stand on this claim tend to be ostracized for wanting to walk a different path, or for bobbing our heads to a different beat. We're looked down upon for our incessant need to chase our passions instead of a career that may line our pockets but ultimately fails to light the fire in the depths of our souls.

Somewhere along the way, our natural desire to dream, and to act on those dreams, is suppressed, and we are told to live a life that hundreds of millions (possibly billions) have already lived. A life where we ultimately settle on the path of least resistance, one we will most likely regret in a retirement home many years from now, but for the time being is safe, and safe is good.

For many of us, when we first talked about our dreams as children, we received a toothy smile and were told we had a "vivid imagination" or "anything is possible," but as the years passed, that turned into "be realistic" or "grow up."

I want to believe that the people who tell us these things do so because they fear for our well-being and are scared we may fail and end up on the street, begging for change or shelter. Of course, there are exceptions, there are those who wish to crush our dreams solely because they themselves were too afraid to take a leap of faith. Yet for the most part, I think those who rain on our parades genuinely care.

However, as noble as the gesture may seem to them, it's detrimental to our development. It causes us to fear failure, to the point where we psych ourselves out before we even try. If we sense even the smallest amount of risk, we seriously consider throwing in the towel.

Failure is not something to be feared but embraced. Without a healthy respect and appreciation for it, we end up filling our lives with mountains of "What ifs" and "I wish I hads."

Embrace Failure

When I was in the fifth grade, about 11 years ago, my life changed. I discovered two of my true passions: basketball and writing. Early on, writing took a backseat to basketball because it wasn't nearly as glamorous.

If I'm going to be honest (one of my main goals with this blog), I have to admit I was atrocious when I first picked up a basketball, and all my detractors (haters) were right to say the things they did.

However, what they didn't know was that I was willing to give every ounce of my being to make my dream a reality—a mindset we must all cultivate in order to breathe life into our dreams.

My dream at that time was to play at the highest level I could. So after years of early morning shooting drills, gallons of sweat, a few trash cans filled with vomit, some spilled blood, and the occasional outpouring of tears, I eventually made it to Cleveland State University, a Division I school currently playing in the Horizon League.

This journey was filled with some of my highest highs, but what I cherish the most are the two lowest moments of my life (for now) where I was completely broken and lost because I had utterly failed.

There were two times where I found myself on my knees, arms limp at my sides and tears freely flowing down my cheeks as I questioned all my decisions that led me to that point. The first was in high school, where after two years I barely touched the floor; I was well acquainted with the bench. The other was in college, where I failed to make the Xavier basketball team.

In my darkest hours, I turned to God and prayed.

I asked, "Why did you give me such confidence in my abilities, but then allow me to fall so short and vindicate those who doubted me?" It was then that I believe God nudged me and gave me the strength to believe once more. I was struck with a clear, unwavering thought: "I'm still breathing, so there's still a chance."

My next step in both situations is the basis of my belief that failure is success's greatest companion, not nemesis. I transferred high schools, leaving friends I've known since kindergarten, and not only did I go on to be a City All-Star and was mentioned in a couple of newspaper articles, but I had an amazing year at John Hay High School. I formed relationships that still last; my principal and athletic director came to my senior night at Cleveland State.

When I transferred from Xavier to CSU, I fulfilled my dream of playing basketball at the highest level I could reach. Not only did I form a true extended family with my teammates and coaches, but during my time at CSU, my passion for writing was revived and I completed the manuscript for my first novel, a young adult fantasy and first in a trilogy. Imagine *Avatar: The Last Airbender* meets *Harry Potter*.

Our failures bring us closer to our dreams and are necessary because they build the character needed to thrive in the highly competitive and successful environments we someday wish to enter. Learn from your failures, allow them to toughen you, but never give in to the idea that because you failed you're a failure.

It's Our Time

My dream for this blog is to reach as many dreamers as I can, and together we can build a community in which we can all thrive and strive toward our dreams.

This is a call to action: Find Your Passion. Commit yourself to it, and live the life you always envisioned for yourself. Make your dream a reality. The dream you hold closest to your heart, the one you rarely share in public because you fear the side glances and snickers that may follow after you share it. Do not be discouraged. Your vision was not meant for everyone to see, but for you alone.

It's time we take a stand. No more can we allow the term "Dreamer" to have negative connotations, but instead, it must describe someone willing to hold firm to their vision no matter the odds. Someone who does not run from failure and risk but welcomes them with a warm smile and arms outstretched. They realize that they are not just obstacles but crucial stepping stones on the road to success.

I humbly ask you to follow me on my newest dream: my journey to get my first novel published. Along the way, I hope to inspire you to pursue and achieve your dreams no matter the cost.

All I ask are for three simple things:

1. A willingness to dream.

2. An open mind.

3. And the courage to keep moving forward.

A Sit-Down With a Dreamer: Laurie Lazzaro Knowlton

January 22nd, 2015

This is the first installment in my interview series with fellow dreamers.

Recently, I had the privilege of interviewing award-winning children's author Laurie Lazzaro Knowlton, who has been published in the trade, educational, craft, and Christian markets. *Why Cowboys Sleep with Their Boots On* is her best-selling picture book, and it won the Premier Print Award given by Eastman Kodak. It has sold over 45,000 copies since its publication. She is also an international speaker who has addressed students, educators, and writers throughout the United States and Mexico.

Did you ever envision yourself having the success that you had, and currently have, when you first began writing?

LK: No. It was always just one step at a time. The first goal was to get something published, an article or something, and so that's what I sold first. And then the next thing was to sell a book. I was the SCBWI (Society of Children's Book Writers and Illustrators) regional advisor for a long time before I got published, and I watched a lot of people and helped a lot of people get that goal while I was still working for it. It took me 12 years to get published with a book or anything besides church bulletins and stuff like that, you know. [Laughs]

So it took a long time, and it was really one of those things where it wasn't an overnight success by any means. I just really kept working and trying to reach that goal, and once I got one published, it's like, "Oh, my gosh. That was a fluke."

RSV: [Laughs]

LK: Yeah, so it's just like my dad always said, "Success is won in inches." You win in little inches, you know? In little bits, and it all adds up to success, but it's the inches. Getting this and then that, and just keeping your nose to the ground and keep working.

RSV: I couldn't agree more.

What obstacles did you face early on and throughout your career that may have caused you to pause or even reconsider writing as a career?

LK: Well, with not getting published, I kept saying, "Okay, I'm going to give it one more year, and if I don't get published, then that's it. I'll go on to something else." And I had people in my life who just said, "Gosh, you're spending an awful lot of time doing that, and it doesn't seem to be paying off."

But I also had people who kept saying, "Oh, my gosh, you have talent, you're almost there, just keep going." And I'm a firm believer in it takes four things to be successful, and that's God, you've got to be right with him. Tenacity, you cannot give up. If you are weak of heart, this is not the business for you.

RSV: [Nods head in agreement]

LK: Talent, God gave it to you, and you honor Him by using that talent and honing it and perfecting it. Finally, timing. For everything, there is a season. That's what I base my success on.

RSV: I really like those four things.

LK: Thanks.

So I'm assuming that for my next question you're going to say "God," but what do you believe allowed you to overcome the obstacles that you faced?

LK: Well, absolutely God. But I also think…Umm, I was a kid that didn't learn how to read early, I had a lot of learning disabilities, but my mother just never would accept that we weren't brilliant, you know?

RSV: Mm-hmm.

LK: And with my dad, it was the same thing, you just don't give up, you just keep going. "You just keep going, Laurie." And so I think it was their drumming into me that I could do it if I just kept working at it. I also believe, like I said, that God gave me a talent, He wanted me to share it and pass it on. So I would say it's kind of family and my belief system and a good, strong faith.

And building on that question, do you think it's important to have a belief in something greater than yourself in order to reach your dreams?

LK: I do, personally. Yeah, I think very much so. I don't know how people go on when difficult things come along if they don't have a faith in something greater than themselves.

I believe that if it's all about you, why reach? I don't know, to me it all goes hand in hand. God created the world, that's what He did. And He made us in His image, and He passed that creativity onto us. You always hear people say, "Oh, I don't have any talent," and yet there are people who are amazing at organizing things, which is a talent I do not have. They don't think that's a talent, but it absolutely is. There are people that go around with messes everywhere, and can't keep things organized.

So I think that everybody has God-given talents, and the biggest thing is finding what those talents are, and claiming them, and practicing them, and perfecting them, and then sharing them.

Is there anything else you'd like to say to anyone who could be reading this?

LK: I would just say, yes it's difficult. But nothing worth having is easy. And if this is a dream of yours, and if you wake up at night and have to write things down, and if when you're driving along and you get these ideas and…what a wonderful gift God gave us with an imagination, and again we honor that by using that tool, so take it, claim it, learn it, do it. Don't let the naysayers say you can't. If you believe you can, you will. I used to get rejection letters, I have enough to probably wallpaper my whole house, but I knew every "no" got me closer to a "yes."

RSV: [Pumping fist in the air in agreement] Mm-hmm.

LK: I would just say you can't sell something if you don't send it out. Just never, never, never give up, and keep working to ensure you get there.

RSV: That was the last question. Thank you for this interview.

LK: You're welcome, and I just wish you all the luck.

Keep Calm & Enjoy the Journey

January 29th, 2015

There isn't a doubt in my mind that the first step to achieving our dreams is to write them down. Our minds are constantly working, and ideas come and go in seconds, never to be heard from again. Our dreams are not immune to this.

But unlike the hundreds of ideas we have daily that vanish without a fight when our attention shifts from them, our dreams (that are connected to our God-given talents) are a little more resilient. They slip under the surface until something we see or hear, maybe even in passing, drags them back to the forefront of our mind, begging us to act on them.

It takes a certain amount of courage for us to write down our dream. I think it's because once we do, we know we've taken the first step on a long journey of making it a reality. There's something about it staring back at you from a piece of paper that forces our minds to begin to conjure up ways to achieve it. It's the first time our dream is no longer an abstract idea in our head but an obtainable goal.

The first couple of weeks, even months, of the journey are exciting, and the few pitfalls we encounter are easily overcome by our enthusiasm. The fact that we're chasing our dream provides us with a high that no drug could ever hope to emulate, but like everything, it fades. Eventually, ideas don't come as swiftly, the setbacks are a little harder to come back from, and the voice of doubt becomes a little more persuasive.

So how do we fight that?

Personally, I take pictures of the small victories on my journey. Think of it as snapping a photo at a popular tourist attraction while on vacation. It reminds you of good times and gives you hope that you can one day replicate the experience or surpass it. Many of our early triumphs will go unnoticed by just about everyone but us. There most likely won't be a parade or trophy when we check off the first couple of things on our to-do list to achieve our dream, but capturing the moment for ourselves can pay off greatly down the road.

The picture accompanying this post [it was a picture of my apartment floor flooded with sheets of paper] was taken in the summer of 2014, and it's one of my favorite pictures to date. Out of context, it's simply a messy room, which is by no means unusual for me, but this particular mess is quite close to my heart. It was taken moments after I finished editing the first draft of my manuscript, before my first round of peer reviews. I had spent three straight days in my apartment editing. I never left my desk except to use the bathroom, shower, and pay for the occasional pizza so I didn't starve.

It was a big moment for me because two years prior, I had written down my dream to write the first book in my proposed trilogy. It was a long journey. There were times during those two years I didn't write for months because I just didn't know what to write. For example, there is a point in the book where a group of characters must travel to an underwater city. I didn't know how they would get there, how they would breathe down there, or how the underwater city would fit into the world as a whole. For example, what goods would they export and import?

All of that took time to develop, and that picture reminds me that everything comes in due time. If you stick with it and continually chip away at it, eventually you will achieve it. When I lack motivation and the doubts rise up, nearly washing me away, that picture and others like it allow me to stem the tide.

Set it in your mind that the journey is going to be long, but that **doesn't** mean you can't enjoy it.

Remember:

1. Take the first step and write down your dream.

2. Capture the little victories along the way, any way you see fit. Whether it's pictures, videos (also a favorite of mine), or writing it down in a notebook. They serve as great reminders of how far you've come and give you the motivation to go further.

3. No matter the obstacles, don't give up on the journey. It'll be worth it.

How Will You Be Remembered?

February 5th, 2015

We all must face the inescapable truth that we will one day die. The idea of death not only forces us to consider our own mortality but makes us wrestle with tough questions such as: Am I living a life that I'll one day be proud of? If I was made for some greater purpose, am I fulfilling it? Will they remember me when I'm gone?

The questions go on and on, but I think the one that hits closest to home for most of us is: Will they remember me when I'm gone? Or, more simply, What's my legacy?

I mean, let's face it, we all want to be remembered. We all want to believe that what we do and bring to the table is so special that they (whoever they may be) will talk about us fondly when we're gone. But what does it take to build such a legacy?

With his birthday nearing, February 6th, I felt compelled that this post feature Bob Marley, one of my idols. I don't idolize him simply because of our shared Jamaican heritage, but for what he stood for and what he was able to accomplish in such a short amount of time. He died when he was 36 years old in 1981, and yet his presence can still be felt as if he was alive today.

Sadly, it's all too common that when Marley is mentioned, it's only as a dreadhead Rastafari pot smoker with a talent for reggae music. Yes, these things describe Marley, but he was far more than that. The fact he was a freedom fighter who used his God-given gift of music to unite people of all races and spread a message of love, courage, and equality is regularly overlooked. This is a man who, after being shot in an assassination attempt two days before the Smile Jamaica concert in 1976, held in order to help calm the political tensions on the island, marched on stage despite his wounds and performed because his belief in his cause was so strong.

When asked why he still performed, he said:

"The people who were trying to make this world worse are not taking the day off. How can I?"

If that doesn't give you chills, I don't know what will.

Greatness is not achieved by accident. I believe Marley accomplished the feats he did because at some point he realized that death eventually claims us all. Until our time comes, we can either be bold and build a legacy that lasts the test of time, and inspire those around us to do the same, or we can live in fear; constantly worried about what our peers might say and think if we go against the status quo.

Marley didn't care how society viewed him and committed

himself to doing what he believed was right: standing up against apartheid and advocating for the unification of all people. Holding firm to your beliefs isn't easy. I mean, Marley was almost assassinated, but it's a life worth living.

Marley saw a problem and spoke out against it. This made him an oddity, but that's what it takes to make a difference. For the most part, that has been lost on us. We're all so consumed with how people may perceive our actions that we fail to ever act. We have an amazing tool at our fingertips in social media, an outlet where our voices can be heard, but so many of us remain silent because voicing our true opinions may cost us a few followers or a couple of likes. Through our silence, we imprison ourselves and are captives in our own minds.

Marley encouraged us in "Redemption Song" to free ourselves from this mental slavery. It's okay to stand out. Yes, being a part of the crowd is easy and you will never have to worry about being singled out. You'll also never have to worry about being remembered. If that's what you want, then so be it, but don't try to hold down those willing to be different because of your cowardice.

Reminding us that it's okay to love our neighbor, to stand up for what's right, and to believe that love can conquer malice and hatred is Bob Marley's true legacy.

If you want a lasting legacy, then it's up to you to:

1. Be brave, and follow your dreams.

2. Speak out against injustice whenever its shadow darkens

the doorway of the just, and give an encouraging word and smile to whoever you encounter on your way.

3. Embrace the fact that one day, it will all end. Live a life worth being remembered, and it will be.

"The greatness of a man is not in how much wealth he acquires, but in his integrity and his ability to affect those around him positively."

—Bob Marley

Happy birthday and rest in peace, Bob Marley. One love.

Success is No Accident

February 19th, 2015

February has long been one of my favorite months due to one event: NBA All-Star Weekend. It showcases a group of individuals who have not only maximized their God-given gifts but who have also made hundreds upon thousands of untold sacrifices to reach the highest level of their profession. It's a grand spectacle.

But every year, my mind is plagued by the same questions: What does it take to reach the apex of your chosen profession? And what sacrifices must be made?

Honestly, these questions are constantly weaving through my mind and are the culprits behind many sleepless nights. It's not uncommon that I find myself staring at the ceiling until the sun rises, contemplating the possible answers.

There comes a point in life—which I think I'm starting to enter—when it's really tempting to settle. The dream is so vast it's almost overwhelming, and the thought of letting it go crosses our minds more times than not. The road is lonely, and the mountain of sacrifices that must be made is daunting.

It's critical that at this point on our journey we have an honest conversation with ourselves. We have to figure out just how far we are willing to go.

On December 5, 2014, I realized I wasn't doing enough to make my dream a reality. That day, I was forced to do some soul-searching. It concluded with me promising myself, and God, that every day from then on, I would do something productive toward achieving my dream. Every single day, I would put forth the necessary effort to better position myself to live out the vision that's in my head. Committing to this helped break my dream into more manageable pieces.

This is vital to our success. Breaking our dreams down into daily objectives protects us from being swallowed up by our own ambition. I believe we're all blessed, to a certain extent, with the ability to dream and envision the lives meant for us. However, it's up to us to give life to that vision, and in order to do so, we have to be deliberate in our actions.

So I did just that. I decided that in order to get to my ultimate destination, I had to be in the best physical, mental, and spiritual shape of my life. This declaration led me to make the following schedule.

My daily routine has become a period of devotion in the morning, then work, then a workout, and then writing in the evening. The devotion builds my spirit and relationship with God. Coupled with my devotion is a short time spent reading a new book of my choosing to help build my mind. Work then provides me with a necessary financial foundation. Lifting and running prepares me physically. And finally, there's writing, which is my craft and passion.

Since I've started this routine, I've realized sacrifices have to be made. I love chilling, going out, and engaging with people. Anyone who has come into contact with me for any meaningful amount of time could deduce as much. However, it came to my attention that the amount of time I was allocating to those activities was not beneficial to my dream.

I've had to cut back on leisure time and social interactions during the week. I had to limit the time I spent texting and surfing social media. I've had to cut out phone calls unless they dealt with work or writing because they used up too much time. I now mainly use my TV only as background noise. However, this has made the weekends that much more enjoyable. I can fully embrace Friday and Saturday nights because I know I've accomplished the necessary work during the week.

Success is no accident, and I can't stress that enough. It's the result of consistent, deliberate, and focused action. Yes, there is a chance that even if we give our all, we may come up short. But it's that chance that we *won't* that fuels those of us willing to chase our dreams. At least that's what fuels me.

I wake up every morning with a smile on my face. I'm convinced that there's no greater way to spend our lives than pursuing our passions. So find it, chase it, and catch it.

Remember:

1. Find a quiet place and take the time to determine what sacrifices must be made in order for you to live out your dream.

2. Make those sacrifices.

3. "I hated every minute of training, but I said, 'Don't quit. Suffer now and live the rest of your life as a champion.'"

— Muhammad Ali

Ramblings on Life – February 19th, 2014 – 7:18AM

My Beliefs at 22

1. If you want it, you have to go get it.

2. God has a plan and will put you where you need to be.

3. People come and go, even those you once considered irreplaceable.

4. When everything is going wrong, it's easy to see all the worst things, but the good things are also there; you just have to look for them.

5. There is a reason behind all things, even the ones that seem especially random and inexplicable.

6. God will BREAK YOU in order to SAVE YOU.

7. Once you lose hope and/or faith, you've lost sight of what life is all about.

8. Give to others, especially if it's at your own expense.

9. Enjoy the little things; they bring the most joy.

10. When you find someone that's worth it, move Heaven and Earth in order to keep them. However, if they're fighting to leave, let them go.

— R.S. Veira

Why We Must Embrace the Little Things

February 26th, 2015

We love to say, "It's all about the little things," yet we somehow regularly overlook them. We allow ourselves to see the end product of someone else's hard work and assume that it happened overnight because in our society, the ridiculous notion of "overnight success" is an accepted concept.

Nowadays, the way success stories are fed to us, it's easy to believe that great feats simply occur and continue to pile on top of each other like flapjacks. We're told it only takes a single moment of genius and the next thing we know, we're sitting on the couch of *The Tonight Show*. We are sold on the idea that all we have to do is wait for said moment and we'll be swimming in money, cars, clothes, and everything else we associate with success. This is not the case.

Great feats are built on the foundation of innumerable small actions and personal achievements. Many of which we overlook, dismiss, and fail to recognize as the potential launching points for our dreams. Because we have bought into the idea of overnight success, we tend to build up a single event in our minds to the point where we wholeheartedly believe that if we do this one thing right, it will rocket us into the upper echelon of fame and fortune.

So when we do succeed at this event and the success that we imagined is not given to us right away, we tend to believe we failed or that the level of success we imagined is not meant for us. When in reality, this is not true. What we have done is laid the first brick of the foundation on which we will build our dreams. Dreams come to our minds easily enough, but making them tangible is anything but.

Individuals who have realized their dreams and reached the level of success I imagine we're all striving toward have shown they understand this idea through their actions. We just have to be willing to look past the headlines of their achievements and look at the journey that led to them.

Los Angeles Lakers shooting guard Kobe Bryant is an excellent example of this. As polarizing as he may be, you either love him or love to hate him. One thing that cannot be argued is that he has reached a level of success in his profession that few ever do. He did this by accepting the fact that it's all about the little things.

One of my favorite Kobe stories is how one night during Team USA basketball training camp, before the London Olympics, he called up the conditioning coach at 4:15 AM for extra work. The conditioning coach arrived at 4:30 to greet Kobe, who had already been working out. He proceeded to put him through a two-hour conditioning and lifting program, and then they parted ways. The trainer arrived for practice later that morning, around 11 AM, to see Kobe shooting in the gym.

Why We Must Embrace the Little Things

The trainer asked him, "What time did you leave the facility?"

Kobe responded, "Oh, just now. I wanted 800 makes. So yeah, just now."

It was no accident that Kobe dominated the NBA for more than a decade. These obsessive habits have been part of his practice routine since he entered the league. The little things, like holding himself to a higher standard and not simply shooting 800 shots but having the specific goal of making 800 baskets, constructed the foundation that allowed him to be a five-time champion and third on the all-time scoring list.

It's stories like these that inspire me and should inspire us all to give more to our dream every day. Think of our dreams as living entities that must be fed daily. If they don't eat on a consistent basis, they will die. I can only imagine the regret that plagues the hearts of those who look back at their lives wondering what could've been if they hadn't been lazy or fearful.

We must buy into the process. We must believe that the little thing we accomplish today will be an important cog in the great machine that is our dream. Personally, I know that to get where I want to go, I have to first build an audience, so I blog.

It takes me three to four hours every Wednesday night to meticulously edit what I wrote Monday and Tuesday night. I not only have to make sure the right message is conveyed, but the post has to meet a certain standard that I hold myself to every week. Most importantly, it has to have enough heart to potentially inspire someone who may read it.

Simply put, I want to be great at what I do. I want to be a great author, and I want to inspire you to be great. Stop waiting for some grand event that will miraculously make you the person you envision being and start perfecting the little things of your craft. Nobody is walking around making dreams come true.

If you want it, you have to go and get it.

Remember:

1. Stop waiting for your dream to come to you.

2. Dedicate the time to perfect the little things that make up your dream.

3. "It's the little details that are vital. Little things make big things happen."
   — John Wooden

Finding Self-Motivation

March 5th, 2015

It's inevitable that a time will come when our motivation dissipates. We no longer feel compelled to give that extra effort that we were willing to before. This may cause us to fret—when in fact we should rejoice, because in order to experience this, we must have made a great deal of progress.

Basically, we have worked ourselves to the point where we have exhausted our initial bit of motivation and are in need of more. This situation usually occurs right after a big breakthrough. It's a dangerous period of time where we have achieved a major milestone—which required a large withdrawal from our motivational reservoir—and we run the risk of becoming complacent.

For most of us, this motivational reservoir within us has been readily replenished by the doubts of our haters. There's an interesting relationship that exists between dreamers and their naysayers. Without their doubts, we wouldn't have had the necessary motivation to even begin on this journey. However, we are constantly at risk of taking anything they may say too much to heart, which can cripple us.

Our first major success silences many of our doubters, and we have fewer naysayers to draw motivation from. Many of these former detractors made regular deposits into our motivational reservoir, and now that their opinions about us are either neutral, or they have even become our supporters, our reservoir is drying up.

Once we arrive at this part of our journey, we can no longer solely rely on the opinions of others to motivate us, and we have to become self-motivated. It's easy for us to become so focused on proving people wrong that sometimes we forget that their opinions are only tools to achieve our dream, and defying their expectations is the cherry on top—*not* the sundae. We must keep in mind that our main focus should always be to perfect our God-given talents.

So how do we become self-motivated?

I've found the easiest way to provide consistent self-motivation is to create a to-do list reaching four to five years into the future. In an earlier post, I discussed writing down your dreams in order to make them more concrete. This is a similar idea.

After the third major revision of my manuscript for my young adult fantasy novel, I went through a couple of months where I didn't really accomplish much. I had gotten really positive feedback from my first few reading groups, which was to be expected since they were filled with some of my biggest supporters. But it was a meeting I had with an eighth-grader, a key demographic, that made me complacent.

His eyes gleamed when we were discussing the characters and

their motivations. He not only understood the broad themes but the more intricate and nuanced ones. He loved the story, and I felt that I had accomplished something.

In a way, I had. There are many people who say they will write a book, start it, and then never finish it. I finished it. Then there were also those who used to chuckle when I, a Black basketball player, said I wanted to be an author, who then fell silent when I completed a coherent manuscript. My fear of not wanting to fall into the first group and my desire to prove the second group wrong drove me to completion. However, with both major motivations gone, I struggled to take the next step.

So in order to keep moving forward, I made a list of everything I wanted to accomplish in the next four years. I look at it weekly. It's one of the most motivating things I do, and it replenishes my reservoir when it's running dry.

The list reminds me that I have a long way to go and numerous tasks to complete before my dream is realized in its entirety. As of this post, nothing on that list has been crossed off, but by the end of this year, I'm on track to knock off a couple:

1.) Be in the best physical shape of my life—exceeding even when I was playing basketball.

2.) Build an audience/maintain a blog.

Even though the opinions of our haters are a great source to pull from, they alone are not enough to propel us to the heights of our grandest dreams. They will fuel us enough for marginal success, but to reach the highest mountaintops, we have to be self-motivated. Be it through a list of future goals or listening to motivational speeches (another favorite of mine reserved for Monday mornings); we have to find what drives us, makes us tick, and mine it.

It's on us to fill that motivational reservoir within and keep it at the appropriate level. The duty of fulfilling our dreams is on no one else's shoulders but our own.

Remember:

1. Enjoy the fact that you have achieved a certain amount of success and that you now need fresh motivation.

2. Don't become complacent. Find out what makes you tick, and use that to replenish your motivational reservoir.

3. Monitor your motivational reservoir, and make sure it remains full.

There's More to Being a Dreamer than Dreaming

March 19th, 2015

More often than not, I find myself holding conversations with people who have great ideas and dreams for themselves but lack the motivation to act on them. Some of them are lazy, others fearful, and some believe that simply having the dream is enough to make it happen. That the dream will cause itself to materialize before them. It's this last group that really bothers me.

It's that mindset that gives the term "dreamer" a negative connotation. It implies that we are just a group of wishful thinkers waiting around for what we want to fall into our laps instead of the meticulous grinders I know we are. Dreaming by itself will not get the job done. The dream is only the blueprint, and it's up to us to handle the construction.

We are a community of dreamers, and as a community, we are obligated to help one another. In order to do that, we must first address this fallacy where we believe that we don't have to exert too much energy in order to gain the success we yearn for. We think we only have to want it badly enough and it will just happen for us, and it's tempting to believe this because who doesn't want things easy? Who doesn't want to be able to sit back, kick their feet up, and watch as their wildest dreams come together before their eyes?

This idea is sold to us every day. Staples even had a commercial based on a button that, when pushed, made things easier. However, that's a fairytale, and it's one that we all at some point either choose to buy into or don't. Those of us who don't usually had someone—a parent, mentor, or peer—save us by showing us through their actions that nothing meaningful comes easy, nor do we really want it to. For those who didn't have that influence, this is my attempt to reach you.

It was the summer going into my senior year of high school, and I had a goal and dream of how I wanted the coming year to play out. I was transferring schools to play basketball, and I wanted the sacrifice of leaving my friends and all that I had known since kindergarten, to be worthwhile.

I decided that for it to be worth the sacrifice, the following had to happen: I had to get written up in the newspaper a couple of times, win some awards, and get an opportunity to play college basketball.

At the start of that summer, I thought I could achieve this dream by doing the same things I was doing before. I didn't see anything wrong with my workouts, and I concluded that the same routine would lead to different results. This does NOT happen. The same routine will give you the same results. I was setting myself up for failure and disappointment by thinking I could achieve things I never had by doing the same things I had always done.

I believe it was God who directed me to my trainer that summer. I say this because during that time, I constantly prayed that He would order my steps down the path that would lead to the destination I had in mind.

My trainer, Brandon, was my former childhood coach in the rec league at the local YMCA. I happened to run into him one afternoon after playing, and in the midst of our conversation, he explained to me that if I really wanted to make an impact on the court, I would have to *work* like I wanted to make an impact. So he volunteered to help me.

Throughout that summer, we worked out every Tuesday and Thursday morning to fit around the camps I attended and my lifting schedule. For the first few weeks, my face was in the trashcan at seven o'clock every morning. It was exactly what I needed.

That summertime grind enabled me to achieve everything I had dreamed of that next season. I got the articles and awards I hoped for. I also set the foundation for eventually playing in college. To this day, it was one of the most grueling summers of my life, but I loved every second of the rewards it reaped. This was an invaluable change in my mindset and one that I sincerely try to instill in those who are waiting around for something to happen.

If we earnestly grind and take the necessary steps every day, we will undoubtedly shine.

I applaud all those who have had the courage to take the first step and dream, but we are doing ourselves no favors if that is as far as we go. There are a lot of people who want the same things we want, and they're not sitting around waiting for them.

I don't care if your dream is to own a business, swim, write, act, or whatever it may be. It won't happen unless you make it happen. If you have to take classes to hone your craft and you don't have the money, then pick up a nine-to-five. If you have a nine-to-five, then pick up a side-hustle. There's no shame in where you start because *you* know where you're going.

We either work ourselves to exhaustion—believe me, there is no other way—and be the individuals we dreamed of, or we sit on the couch and watch those who did the work live out their dreams on the TV screen.

I can only speak for myself, but I have no plans of watching someone else live my dream.

Remember:

1. Dreamers don't just dream, they DO.

2. The only way to shine is to grind, there is no way around it.

3. If you want things you've never had, you have to be willing to do things you've never done.

Faith

March 26th, 2015

Faith can be defined as being sure of what we hope for, and certain of what we don't see (Hebrews 11:1). It's a simple idea, but it raises a lot of complex emotions. This is due to the fact that it is tied to religion, and anytime religion is discussed, it's a very sensitive conversation. It's important to me that I state that I'm not aiming to force my beliefs on anyone. I think the beauty of our relationship with God is coming to terms with it on our own.

However, the fact of the matter is that faith is our greatest asset on our journey. It's impossible for us to make any significant progress without struggling with it, building it, and understanding it.

Faith is what first gives us the courage to dream. Our journey only began because a small voice within us spoke up and proclaimed that it was possible. That voice we heard was our faith. How far we get on this journey is determined by how we manage that voice. The difference between the people who are living their dreams and those who aren't is that the ones who are listened and nurtured that voice. They heard its cries and took its advice. They decided to walk by faith and not by sight.

Walking by sight refers to the act of allowing our current situations and circumstances to dictate our future success. Our sight is limited. We can only see the present, and when we depend on sight alone, all we see are our current struggles. This causes us to believe that we will never have what we dream of because we can't see it with our eyes. We tell ourselves that our present is too dark, so how can our future be bright?

Walking by faith boils down to the fact that I know I'm struggling right now, *but* I know it will end if I keep pushing forward. Faith allows us to catch a glimpse of our future and gives us the strength to believe that we were given our visions and dreams because we have the capacity to make them a reality. Faith fuels us to grind even when we can't see the fruit of our labor right away, and when we eventually harvest the fruit of said labor, our faith uses it as nourishment and grows. The greater our faith, the greater the dream we can accomplish.

When I first transferred high schools, few considered it a good idea. Initially, they thought I was making a mistake. I don't blame them, because my decision was based on faith and not concrete facts. That's hard for people who don't share the vision to understand.

It was a lonely time. All I had was my faith in God, which was nowhere near as strong as it is now. At that point in my life, my faith was only a small voice that periodically whispered, "You can do it." That was it, and nothing more. I never felt so isolated. Nonetheless, during that period of isolation, I toiled away in the gym. The fruit of that labor did not come for months. All I had for comfort while I sowed my seeds was that small voice, and I rallied behind it.

So when everything I had dreamed of came to fruition and I harvested the fruit of my labor, my faith feasted and grew.

When I transferred colleges to continue chasing my dream, it was again not a popular decision among those close to me. However, this time the voice was no longer whispering. It had a little more bass and a little more confidence. It said, "You will do this." So again I rallied behind it. I toiled away and sowed my seeds.

When my basketball career ended and I had finished playing Division I basketball, my faith again dined on the fruit of my labor and grew. With basketball over, the dream of being a successful novelist was brought back to the forefront of my mind. Now the voice was no longer meek. It was no longer speaking with just a little confidence. It was boldly shouting, "Why not?"

Naturally, as my leaps of faith continued to pan out, those who had reservations about how I was making decisions began to support me, which was nice. But in all honesty, their support was no longer a necessity. The trials and tribulations I had navigated revealed to me that with my faith backing me, I could accomplish anything. I had no more reason to fear or cling to the opinions of others.

I thank God for the struggles and ask for more. They may break me momentarily, but when I come back, my faith and I will be stronger because of it, and I will be that much closer to the dream.

It's not easy living by faith. It will cause us to be misunderstood, but we're used to that because we're dreamers. The strength of our faith and the likelihood of us achieving our dreams are directly correlated. Those with little faith will see little results. They will be the first to put us down and call us unrealistic or idealists. But they are wrong. Faith is as real as it gets. It's no fantasy.

When we are weak and alone, it is from our faith that we will draw strength. We *have* to have faith in something bigger than us because the journey is too long and treacherous to do it alone.

Feed your faith, and you will feed your dream.

Remember:

1. The greater our faith, the greater the dream we can accomplish.

2. Our faith and our dreams go hand in hand.

3. "We live by faith, not by sight."
    — 2 Corinthians 5:7

Doubt

April 2nd, 2015

It's only logical to follow up last week's post on faith with one focused on doubt. The two are yin and yang. We can't discuss one without exploring the other. Like all things that are closely related, they have their striking similarities and glaring differences.

Like faith, *we* determine how strong and great doubt can become. Also like faith, it affects us all. No matter how successful or unsuccessful we are, doubt will find us. Unlike faith, when doubt grows, it does not fill us with courage but robs us of it. Doubt is a virus, and like all viruses, if left unchecked, it can be lethal.

There are four stages to this virus. The first stage is when we are infected. This commonly takes place before we take on a major risk, or right after any type of success. Common carriers of the infection are the things we hear someone say about us or our dream, the things we read directed toward us or our dream, and the times we allow ourselves to overthink.

Once infected, we begin to get small inklings that cause us to ponder if we're really as talented, as intelligent, or as strong as we had believed. The virus feasts on these insecurities. It then grows and spreads throughout our minds.

In stage two, we will find ourselves uttering phrases like, "I'll try it next time," or "I'm probably not good enough to do this anyway," even though days or even hours before, we had the utmost faith in our ability and dream. At this stage, we haven't yet completely stopped working toward our dream, but our progress has slowed tremendously. The virus has completely clouded our judgment. It has forced us to believe that we aren't actually doubting ourselves—we are just being "realistic."

In stage three, we have reached complete inactivity. We avoid all thoughts of our dream and steer conversation away from it at all costs. The virus has robbed us of the enthusiasm and passion that once gushed from every pore of our bodies when we presented our dream to others. Excuses become second nature to us. We find any reason, no matter how small or trivial, to avoid making any positive progress toward our dream. We have concluded that it would be easier and safer for us to take the path most traveled. In stage four, the virus kills and consumes the dream. The dream is buried with little fanfare and we gladly leave it behind, only to live out our lives with deep, unrelenting regret.

This virus's ravenous appetite is only appeased after it has sufficiently debilitated us, but all hope is not lost. I am a survivor of doubt. A few years ago, I was struck with a rather severe case of writer's block 50 pages into my manuscript. In order to give myself a break, I focused on other things. I began doing research on the publishing industry and pursuing a career as an author. My preliminary research turned up far more negative things than good.

The first issues I came across were the inconsistent pay, the difficulty of landing an agent, and the likelihood of becoming a starving artist. These things were scary. This, coupled with my writer's block, gave the virus a foothold.

I soon found myself writing even more sparingly. More often than not, I was watching TV after basketball practice instead of honing my craft. I began to tell myself that I'd do double the work the next day, only to find myself repeating the process the following day. It wasn't long before I was completely inactive. I didn't write for months. It was at this time I realized the dangers of my predicament. Luckily, before the virus could reach stage four, I forced myself to make one last stand. I did more thorough research.

After digging deeper, I discovered what I needed. I found stories upon stories of authors who had similar trouble. Individuals who had almost succumbed to their doubt but instead clung to whatever faith they had and pushed through. Doubt caused Stephen King to throw away the manuscript for his classic novel *Carrie*. His wife pulled it out of the trash and told him to give it another try. The rest is history.

I took these stories to heart and went on a writing rampage. I dedicated myself to writing every day until I finished. Any day I felt myself slipping, I rallied behind the voice of my faith that had grown from my previous struggles. I finished my manuscript within the following year.

There is no cure for doubt. There is only a temporary remedy provided by our faith. Our battle with doubt is not a one-time event, and it will continue throughout our lives. I've had numerous other close calls, including the initial launch of this blog and the weekly encounters that come with every post. However, through my faith, I am able to keep doubt at bay.

Dreamers fall victim to doubt every day. As dreamers, we must support one another by sharing our own stories of triumph over doubt. Through our testimonies, we can help strengthen one another's courage to take risks, which in return collectively builds our faith. Yes, we are on our own God-given paths and journeys that were designed for only us to complete. However, that does not mean we are alone. We are united by our common passion to see our dreams realized.

The saddest event in a dreamer's life is to bury the dream due to doubt. That is the one funeral in our lives we have the power to prevent, and it's our responsibility to do so.

Remember:

1. Doubt will only claim our dream if we let it.

2. Our faith is our only weapon against doubt; we must build it up.

3. "Doubt kills more dreams than fear ever will."

— Suzy Kassem

Ramblings on Life – October 15th, 2014 – 11:00PM

I feel my mind is constantly at war between the person I strive to be, the person I am, and the person I used to be.

— R.S. Veira

A Sit-Down With a Dreamer: Rich Morrow

April 9th, 2015

This is the second installment in my interview series with fellow dreamers.

While in Los Angeles last week, I had the chance to catch up and have a sit-down with an old friend, Rich Morrow. He was a basketball player at Florida Atlantic University. He has recently left the hardwood behind to focus on a career in acting, writing, and producing. He has gathered an impressive following on both Instagram (*@Rich.Official*) and Vine (*@Richboy*) due to his acting prowess and modeling exploits.

What events do you believe put you on the journey you're embarking on right now? What put it all into motion?

RM: What set me up? Everything, honestly. I don't think you could ever pinpoint it to one exact thing when you feel like you're living with purpose, because it's a combination of everything that you've gone through. So I would say it started out when I was younger, very, very young. I was always the kind of kid that learned things by example. So watching TV and sports and everything like that, that's kind of what drove me to want to play sports and want to be in front of the camera and all of that good stuff.

Once I got to high school, I made the decision that I was going to go with basketball. I put everything that I could into it. It became everything to me, and I made that dream come true.

That's kind of where I would say it really started—accomplishing that first dream that I set for myself. If you put in the work, and if you can get a taste of what it feels like to accomplish a dream or something that you pictured for so long, it just makes you fearless.

RSV: [Nods head] I completely agree.

So you started acting and modeling. Those two things are daunting ventures by themselves. What do you believe allowed you to overcome the initial doubt that you faced when you first started?

RM: That's a good question . . . it was probably a talk I had with myself. I was very, very doubtful about a lot of things. You look at the pool of people that you are in competition with, and it's pretty much endless. But at the same time, I looked myself in the mirror and I was thinking about all the things that really drive me and the things that I wish I could have. Just everything. It's almost like dreaming out loud. And I would actually talk to myself. It's different when you're just thinking about things. When you actually hear it out loud, it's almost like it makes it real. That's like the first step in making it a reality.

RSV: Absolutely.

RM: So I would actually talk to myself and just let it all out. Once I was able to do that, then I felt comfortable. I said to myself: "You know what, this is my life. This is what I feel like my purpose is. Why would I let anything hold me back from that?"

I started making Vines and building a following. I was in college, and I started to get a buzz around town. So it built my confidence up, but at the same time, it was nothing compared to what I knew I really wanted out of this if I was going to take it seriously.

So I had to take that next step. I told myself: "I'm going to be an actor one day." And the more I said it, the more real it became to me. Then I started to figure out what I would need to do in order to make this happen. I don't want to half do anything, that's not me. If I'm going to do something, why not be the greatest at it?

RSV: True, anybody can be ordinary, it's easy.

RM: Exactly. If you're going to do it, be great.

Are you ever anxious about your future, about what's coming for you? How do you manage that?

RM: Every single day. I get very anxious. But at the same time, I'm like: "Okay, you know what, this is all part of the journey." I want to be able to look back on my journey and appreciate it. It's just going to make it all sweeter when it does happen. It doesn't matter how long it takes, because the payoff is going to be everything. It's going to be everything that you dreamed of this whole time.

RSV: It's all about the journey.

RM: It really is. You have to appreciate the journey because there's beauty in it. J. Cole really said that right, because that's the only way you learn. You don't just jump to that dream character you picture yourself as. The journey is the part of your dream that you don't see. You don't see the struggle that it takes to get there. You just see the end result.

Exactly. You mentioned God earlier. How big of a role do you feel He's played in your journey?

RM: The biggest role. Honestly, I don't put anything above Him. I truly believe that although we make our own decisions, He is always the one who guides me wherever I go. And I love Him for that because I have never felt like He wasn't there. If you really, really believe in things, things start to attract to you. I really believe that, and it was like the moment that I decided I wanted to be an actor, it was like something shifted in the universe.

People would see me out, and usually they would ask, "Oh, what sport do you play?" because I look like an athlete. Well, after I made that decision, as crazy as it sounds, people would come up to me and be like, "Do you model?" or "What do you do?"

And I'm like, "What do I do? What do you mean what do I do?" I wasn't used to people asking me that. That's when it started to change. I just laugh because I'm like, "God has a sense of humor." [Laughs]

RSV: [Laughs] He does.

RM: He just does great things, and I know without Him I wouldn't be where I am, because the faith that I have in Him pushes me through so much I would not be able to go through myself. It really does push me, because I always feel like He's watching.

We are ambitious dreamers, and our dreams are usually so big that they're frightening, even paralyzing. What advice do you have for others like us when it comes to taking that first step and pursuing the dream?

RM: When it comes down to taking that first step, I think that you have to be honest with yourself. If you're nervous or afraid, tell yourself that, "Okay, I'm nervous about this journey." But if you do believe in God, you should know that God is always going to have your back regardless.

You got to be realistic. Realistic is probably the best word that I can give people that have huge dreams. Some things may not seem realistic, to be honest. But at the same time, being realistic forces you to find the necessary steps to get where you want to go. You're being realistic in the sense that you are creating a path.

So you have to do your research, and you have to learn. Once you start to learn, you start to learn exactly the steps that need to be taken. You find out who the best ones in your field are and how they got there. That's where you start at, because everybody thinks that people just jump to success.

RSV: They do.

RM: They don't jump to success. They worked for it for a very, very long time before anybody even knows them. I would tell the dreamer, "Keep dreaming, you have to keep dreaming." But then you have to transition that dreaming into dreaming out loud, then you have to transition that dreaming into action, and you really, really, really have to believe it. It is one thing to dream, but it's another thing to believe in it.

You have to believe in your dream, you have to believe in yourself, you have to believe that you're capable of doing it.

RSV: I couldn't agree more. So that's really all I got, man. I appreciate it.

RM: No problem, man. I love talking to you, you already know. Conversations with a dreamer.

RSV: Yessir.

How to Beat a Slump

April 23rd, 2015

We all go through slumps—a period of time where even though we're doing all the right things, nothing seems to go as planned. Things are just off. Slumps can occur out of nowhere, and if we don't pay attention, we can miss the signs that one is on the horizon. They slowly build, a couple of "off-days" turn into weeks, which eventually turn into months. If adjustments aren't made, the situation will continue to worsen.

When it was time to write this post, I felt especially motivated because I knew working on this piece would help to pull me out of my current slump. Over the last few weeks, I've noticed that I was getting the writing I needed to do done, but I was pushing it off until I absolutely had to do it. I was no longer working on my craft daily. This was a clear sign I was entering a slump, and I had to re-examine my routine.

Some of the best advice I ever received about handling slumps was during my time playing basketball. I'm a shooter, that's always been my basketball identity. The thing about shooting is that if you don't stay on top of it, it's easy to fall out of rhythm. One of my earliest coaches used to tell me: "Shooters shoot, never stop shooting."

I fully embraced that, because I also loved to score. However, it wasn't until I grew older that I fully understood the phrase. My coach wasn't only referring to shooting in a game, but all the time. If I truly identified as a shooter, then I should've been regularly putting up shots outside of games.

Practicing your craft builds good habits, muscle memory, and deters slumps.

During my senior year of high school, I went on a scoring tear where for a string of games, I couldn't miss. Before that stretch, I was in the gym shooting whenever I could. I got shots up before and after practice. I would even go to the gym during free periods. I was always shooting.

However, once that stretch began, I was no longer practicing like I had been before. Shortly after that string of games, I found myself in a serious slump. My shot and touch were off, and I never recovered that season. This contributed to my team's early postseason exit.

From that experience, I realized how dangerous complacency can be. I had reached a level of success that I was happy with, and I relaxed. My own complacency greatly raised my chances of falling into a slump. Slumps are a part of life, but we can lessen their occurrence and duration by avoiding complacency and by continuously honing our craft.

The worst part about a slump is that, while in the midst of one, it's nearly impossible to see the end. They're mentally sapping, depressing, and cause us to feel isolated. We go searching for answers when *the* answer has been there all along. The key to recovery is remembering what got us to where we were before in the first place.

To remedy my current slump, I had to keep writing. Especially when I didn't feel like it. The steady stream of ideas that usually flowed through my mind had somehow been dammed up. I discovered that continuing to write was the best way to remove the obstruction.

I didn't have to write anything amazing or even great, I just had to write. For example, I honestly don't believe this post is a great representation of my work, but I had to finish it, not just for me but to show that, even in slumps, we must find a way to produce. By doing that, we will free ourselves.

While writing this post, I could feel the dam giving way. With each sentence, a fresh crack appeared and a couple of new ideas slithered through. As of writing this, I'm still not free, but I'm on my way.

Slumps, like everything, are temporary. If we are determined, have faith, and are unwilling to yield, there is nothing to worry about. We should actually look at them as a pat on the back. In order to have one, we had to have found some success beforehand.

Remember:

How to Beat a Slump

1. Slumps happen to everyone.

2. Avoid complacency, and you will lessen your chances of falling into a slump.

3. Revert to the actions that allowed you to reach success, tweak it if you must, and then lose yourself in it again.

What I Learned in Third Grade

April 30th, 2015

Developing humility is a painful process. When someone describes "a humbling experience," it usually isn't painted as an enjoyable one. In most cases, it involves us coming to terms with the fact that we are not as amazing as we have led ourselves to believe. As unpleasant as that may sound, I believe humility is the key to sustained success.

Humility is a difficult concept to embrace because we love to revel in our own press clippings. Who doesn't like to have their ego stroked? When we hear our peers, especially those we admire, sing our praises, it's hard not to buy into the hype.

There's nothing wrong with feeling good about ourselves. In fact, there's a certain level of confidence that we have to have in order to achieve our dreams. We run into a problem when that confidence turns into arrogance. Arrogance can best be described as confidence on steroids. While confidence is a calm self-assurance, arrogance is a boisterous "look at me and what I can do" attitude.

I can only smile when I reminisce on my younger days, a time when I was far more arrogant than confident. It was this arrogance that led to one of the defining moments of my life. It occurred at my birthday party in the third grade.

For my birthday that year, I decided to have a Super Smash Bros. one-on-one tournament. Super Smash Bros. is a game where you take your favorite Nintendo characters and engage in an all-out brawl, a fight to the death. For example, you could have Mario vs. Pikachu, or Link vs. Donkey Kong, etc.

My cousin and I invested months into this game. Since we played it to such an extent, and the game was a really popular one at the time, I thought it would be a great idea to have a tournament for my birthday. Who doesn't want to beat up on their friends and reign supreme on their *birthday*?

Leading up to the big day, I told anyone who would listen that it would take a miracle for me to lose. I was Ali before a big fight. My tongue was writing checks that I had no doubt my virtual fists would cash.

Unfortunately, I did not realize that I was only highly skilled with one character, Fox McCloud. I simply assumed that since I was so good with him, my skill would translate to any other character.

The night before my birthday, my cousin and I were up late preparing and we happened to unlock the secret character Luigi. In my excitement and arrogance, I decided that since my cousin always played as Mario, it would be cool to have a Mario vs. Luigi final to end the tournament. I tossed aside Fox and entered the tournament with Luigi.

The next day, I was pummeled in the first round by someone I had no business losing to. My cousin went on to win it all.

It was devastating.

Not only did I have to sit through the movie afterward with a sour look on my face, but I had to endure the endless taunting,

"We thought you were sooooo good, Raph?"

It was a humbling experience. Now, what did I learn from this?

I learned arrogance is a stench. Its fumes signal those in the vicinity that this individual has lost himself in his own success. He now believes that he is greater than he actually is. He has forgotten that his talent is a blessing from God and should be treated as such.

If we are as good as we believe, our performance will speak for itself. There's no reason to be prideful or boastful. It's important that as we continue to accumulate successful ventures, we manage our egos. We must be careful that our confidence never evolves into arrogance, because while confidence tends to attract, arrogance acts as a repellent.

Make no mistake about it, we do not know everything. On the journey to our dream, we will need the help and guidance from those who have gone before us. They will be more willing to point out potential pitfalls to those who are humble. No one wants to help someone who acts like they know it all.

Our attitude toward success, and how we carry ourselves when we achieve it, not only affects how others see us but our ability to collaborate and learn from them.

Remember:

1. There's nothing wrong with confidence, but don't let it become arrogance.

2. Let your actions speak for you.

3. "Humility is the true key to success. Successful people lose their way at times. They often embrace and overindulge from the fruits of success. Humility halts this arrogance and self-indulging trap. Humble people share the credit and wealth, remaining focused and hungry to continue the journey of success."
— Rick Pitino

I also wanted to let everyone know that my Facebook Author Fan Page just hit 1,000 likes last week, and I really appreciate all the support. I would also really love to interact more with the people that read and subscribe to my blog. Don't be shy, leave a comment or hit me up on Twitter. I love getting to meet and know other dreamers.

Watch the Company You Keep
May 7th, 2015

We all need someone. Contrary to popular belief and the "one man against the world" stories we hear, no one does it alone. We need someone, or a group of individuals, who will help us along on our journey. They are the ones who pick us up when we fall and who lean on us when they stumble. They transcend friendship and become something more. They become a part of us, and we become a part of them.

These bonds are forged through shared struggle and pain. Together, you've seen the darkest pits of despair and promised to always be willing to pull one another from their grasp, no matter the lengths. These relationships are built on trust.

Picture a wolf pack. Each member looks out for one another. If one eats, then they all eat. All members of the pack share a common goal: survival. The individuals that form your pack must share the common goal of success.

These individuals grow to know you nearly as well as you know yourself. You push each other to be better than you thought possible and inspire one another to never give up. It's rather simple.

There's a shared understanding that a group of determined, like-minded individuals can make the infeasible feasible.

How do you find the members of your pack?

Honestly, I don't exactly know. However, I believe the first step to finding them is to make a conscious decision to surround yourself with like-minded individuals. Not yes-men, but like-minded.

Yes-men (or women) will agree with you no matter your decision, while like-minded individuals will challenge you when they are unsure of your conclusions or plans. When we no longer put up with yes-men and those who take from us but never give back, we elect to chase the dream that God has instilled in us. That's when He flanks us with the individuals needed to make it a reality.

I'm blessed to have found my pack. We're bonded by our shared belief in each other.

As I've talked about before, during my first couple of years of high school basketball, I didn't play much. What I didn't mention was the young man who sat with me at the end of the bench and no matter the circumstance, continued to say, "I believe in you, Raph."

It was this same young man who kept me company for hours after practice while I shot in the gym. The same one who continued to believe in me when everyone doubted my decision to transfer, in both high school and college. And the same one who, when I told him I wanted to be an author, smiled and said, "I believe in you."

The young man's name is Will, and he is more than a best friend. He shares a rare space in my heart reserved for the few other steadfast individuals that God has lovingly blessed me with on this journey. However, I single him out in this post because he is the epitome of what I'm trying to explain. He was my friend in the dark when all those who claimed they supported me disappeared. For that, I will always stand by his side and have the utmost respect for him.

The key to such a friendship is mutuality. I fully support his dreams, as he supports mine. To develop the type of bond I'm describing, earnest support must be reciprocated. There should never be a time where a member of your pack, squad, or crew (however you wish to describe it) feels isolated. If this ever occurs, then the focus must temporarily shift from personal goals to the health of your fallen comrade.

However, many of us are surrounded by people who claim to be that truest friend, when in reality it's nothing more than a façade. We believe their claims, and when they fall, we stop focusing on our goals to tend to them. Yet in return, they neither look out for us nor aim to better themselves, but instead start to see us as a crutch. They abuse and exploit the friendship. It's these individuals that we must weed out. It won't be easy.

They tend to be those who have been with us since childhood or for many years. Letting them go causes us to feel more like Brutus than Caesar, but if we allow them to bring us down, we betray ourselves.

I know this is not a simple thing that I ask, but we must distance ourselves from the friends or family members that use us because they know we will always bail them out. It's only then that the true friends, like Will, become obvious. It's only then that we can begin to form the pack, squad, or crew that will not only allow us to achieve our dreams but allow them to achieve theirs, as well.

The ultimate goal is to look out for those we care for, but that can't happen if we constantly look out for those who only care for themselves. We must remove ourselves enough from them so that they no longer run in our pack. However, stay close enough so we can respond to a *true* cry for help.

We are the company that we keep. If we only hang around lazy, selfish, unmotivated individuals who are satisfied with mediocrity, what are we saying about ourselves?

To reach our dreams, our pack must consist of others who are aiming for theirs.

Remember:

1. Your pack consists of those closest to you. Make sure those individuals are building you up and not tearing you down.

2. We have to distance ourselves from those who refuse to grow with us.

3. "A friend loves at all times, and a brother is born for adversity."
   — Proverbs 17:17

Season Finale

May 21st, 2015

I guess it's cliché to say that while attending my friend Landen's graduation all I could think about was the future, but that's exactly what happened. To be more precise, it wasn't the future I was fixated on but the changes that were occurring all around me that I was suddenly aware of.

I graduated in December of last year, but it wasn't until last weekend that it really sank in that everything was going to be different. I like to think of life as a TV series; our lives are divided up into seasons. This was a season finale, and a new season was around the corner.

I began to wonder about the new adventures I would embark on and the new people I would meet along the way. New rivals, love interests, and friends. It then dawned on me how much I had changed from the beginning of this season to now.

Change is scary, because there's no way to predict exactly how the cards will fall when the winds of change settle down. It's natural to be nervous, but it's not something we should fear. When we're in the midst of a transition, we're supposed to be uncomfortable. That uncomfortableness forces us to try new things, learn new talents, and that leads to growth.

If we cling to the past and what was, we rob ourselves of the opportunity of enjoying an unforeseen, fulfilling future.

My journey to playing college basketball really helped to facilitate my growth over this last season of my life. It began in a hallway at Xavier University, where I first ran into Landen. We had both come for a visit, neither of us looking to play basketball anymore, and we met while I was waiting outside the Registrar's office.

We talked for a moment, mentioned we had both played basketball in high school, exchanged numbers, and that was it. It was nothing more than that.

Fast-forward to the first day we arrived on campus in the fall. We met up, and again we didn't talk much, but we managed to make plans to wake up at 5 AM the next morning to shoot around on the outside basketball courts and run through a couple of drills.

That morning, we both silently realized that we each wanted to walk-on to the basketball team, and we also recognized we were each other's biggest competition.

Landen and I laugh about it now, but that competition for a spot on the team led us to be rivals in everything we did. It ranged from who could provide the best haircuts to video games, academics, and to even who could get the most girls.

It was a strange friendship, because even though we hung out a lot and lived together for half of sophomore year, we rarely spoke to each other. Whenever it was just us in a room, we sat in absolute silence, minding our own business, locked in mental warfare.

The point of this story is to illustrate change. **How a rival became a best friend.**

Landen and I forced one another out of our comfort zones. The key to meaningful change is learning to thrive outside of such zones. Once outside, we had to adapt to being uncomfortable. We had to learn and develop new tactics to survive.

The growth that resulted from that struggle ultimately allowed us both to play Division I basketball, him at Xavier and me at Cleveland State. We pushed each other to be the best we could be. What *more* could you ask for from a friend?

It was Landen beating me for that spot at Xavier that taught me that even after giving it your all, you can still fail. **However**, if we take the time to recognize the skills we have gained during the journey leading up to that failure, it becomes abundantly clear that we are now equipped to travel farther than we ever imagined.

That failure set the rest of my life in motion. It allowed me to play at CSU, start and finish my manuscript, and then begin this blog. It allowed me to unearth my true passion.

Four years ago, at the start of this season of my life, an ending like this would've been inconceivable—that I would voluntarily drive four hours to celebrate the graduation of one of my biggest rivals who became one of my best friends. It's amazing what can happen when we embrace change.

It occurred to me while I was considering all this that I had settled into a *new* comfort zone and that this graduation signaled that change was coming. I'll soon be cast from comfort. I'll again take my lumps and bruises, but it helps to view it as a necessary inconvenience on the journey to achieve my dreams.

Every new season brings a few new cast members and a new set of obstacles. These new changes are meant to prepare us, not break us. When we fight change, it's because at some level we have lost faith in God and no longer believe things will turn out well for us.

We must smile when change approaches and greet it like an old friend. We shouldn't want to be the person we were four years ago, nor should we want to be the person we are currently four years from now.

When we finally reach that *series finale* in which we achieve our dreams, it will have only been possible because we are the sum of all the skills we acquired from embracing the changes.

Remember:

1. Change can be messy, but it's necessary.

2. You either remain comfortable and settle or be uncomfortable and thrive.

3. "If there is no struggle, there is no progress."

— Frederick Douglass

Ramblings on Love – November 21st, 2016 – 2:39AM

Some of my deepest revelations have come because of women. It's the medium through which I think God reaches me best. It's the vessel that's most likely going to make it to port with the least amount of resistance. A cute girl with a slim waist has always been the best messenger. I wonder if that will always be the case.

— R.S. Veira

Passion, Where Art Thou?

May 28th, 2015

A familiar hum is in the air. It's about that time of the year when countless commencement speeches are given around the country urging high school and college graduates to follow their passions. Yet even though this message is prevalent, it seems to go unheeded.

I think the cause behind this disconnect is that the majority of the listeners have no idea what they're truly passionate about. Graduates listen to speakers eloquently elaborate on their past hardships and victories in an attempt to arouse the graduates' spirits to the point where they throw caution to the wind and follow their passions. But it's a futile endeavor if the graduates have no idea how to identify their passions to begin with.

Having given speeches of this nature and heard countless more, I've had the opportunity to experience both sides, and I've been able to draw the following conclusion.

Discovering what we're passionate about is not nearly as daunting a task as we might believe.

One of the main reasons finding our passions can seem like a chore is because initially, we can't imagine any activity that we could love *so* wholeheartedly. Witnessing others express immense enthusiasm for their craft can be intimidating. It forces us to think, "Do I love doing anything like that?" And if we are unable to adequately respond to this question, we reason that we must have no talent to be passionate about.

This is not the case. It's honestly the furthest thing from the truth. God blessed us all with talent. Admittedly, some of us are more talented than others, but nonetheless, we are all blessed with a gift. The duty falls on us to acknowledge this talent and then develop it.

So how can you find your passion?

In fifth grade, I was friends with a kid who absolutely loved video games. His passion for them was nearly tangible. Now, I considered myself quite the video game enthusiast, but my enthusiasm was laughable compared to his passion. The way he described one particular game, *Gauntlet Dark Legacy*, was so enthralling that it immediately jumped to the top of my birthday wish list.

While I impatiently waited for my birthday to arrive, I would spend my free time during the school day listening to him explain his latest adventure. I applaud him for putting up with me, because I obsess over the small details of a story. It was common for me to interrupt him and ask him to go back and explain his triumph again, but in excruciating detail. He never flinched and almost seemed to relish the opportunity.

At the time, I wondered if I would ever be able to love anything with such vigor. Little did I know, that coming winter I would start playing basketball, and the following spring I would write my first short story. I knew these were my passions because of the emotions they brought forth. Whenever they were discussed, I could do nothing to stop the joy that rose up from the pit of my stomach. I was powerless to quell the storm of emotions that swirled in me when I was asked to verbalize my passions. Just ask me about my thoughts on arguably the greatest basketball player of all time, Kobe Bryant.

Our passions can be identified when we allow ourselves to remember what we enjoyed doing before we were told what we should enjoy doing. For the most part, this means venturing back to when we were children. A time where our happiness trumped our fear of being judged.

Once we have found the activity, we must allow ourselves to play with the frightening idea of doing that activity full-time. This can be a scary idea since some of our passions can lie in obscure things or in activities that aren't mainstream. The question we must ask ourselves is: How can this activity that brings me unparalleled joy be used to sustain my future?

It's a difficult question. The answer will most likely reveal a path much different from the one traveled by the majority of your peers. Chasing our passions can cause us to go against the status quo, and that can be horrifying no matter our age. However, we were not created to be meek. We were not meant to shuffle around with our heads down, following the masses, afraid to look up because of what the person next to us may say or think.

We were created to be bold and courageous. We each harbor the ability to inspire our peers and all who encounter us. But to do that we must decide to develop our God-given talents and pursue our passions.

The struggle is not in finding our passion; the struggle is in deciding if we're going to follow it.

Remember:

1. We all have something we're passionate about. Embrace it.

2. Forge your own path.

3. "Passion is one great force that unleashes creativity, because if you're passionate about something, then you're more willing to take risks."
— Yo-Yo Ma

A Sit-Down With a Dreamer: Antonio Veira

June 4th, 2015

This is the third installment in my interview series with fellow dreamers.

I recently had the opportunity to sit down and catch up with my big brother, Antonio Veira. He is not only the kitchen manager at the popular Blue Point Grille in Cleveland, OH, but a major inspiration and blessing in my life. Despite dealing with a period of incarceration and the passing of his grandmother (we share the same father but different mothers), he has been able to rise above it all and pursue his dreams.

As a kitchen manager, what are your responsibilities?

AV: I'm a leader amongst the cooks. I manage the kitchen alongside the sous chef and executive chef. I have different responsibilities. I oversee sanitation, make sure the food goes out correctly, and manage the line.

Is your current career what you dreamed of doing when you first started seriously contemplating your future?

AV: Yeah, I really got serious about things when I was 20. I realized I was good with food, and creative. I was just real into it because cooking is like a science. I like science. The only science I'm probably good at. So I just decided to go that route. Anything you realize you're good at, you need to pursue.

I was about 20 when I decided to go to culinary school. Papa [our father] actually kind of brought up the idea and helped make it happen. I went to Italy, and I went from there.

While you were in Italy, did anything happen that made it clear that cooking was what you needed to do?

AV: Not when I was in Italy, per se. I'd say after Italy. Probably after I got out of jail and I was working at the Mad Greek up in Cleveland Heights as a sous chef. That's where I kind of built myself up as a leader and a manager. Developing recipes and carrying out good work. I was praised for it consistently and it clicked in my head, maybe I should pursue a career.

You mentioned jail. Is that the biggest obstacle you faced when you were trying to become a chef?

AV: No. Not as far as becoming a chef. To be honest, when I was in the joint, I didn't really think about my future at all. I was thinking about the present. Talk about one of the hardest things in my life. That and losing my grandmother at 20, because she was like my mom. She helped raise me.

It was real tough. Those two things are the toughest things in my life that I have been through so far. But they didn't really stop my career. My grandmother passing, though, actually gave me inspiration to make myself into something just for her. It kind of lit a fire up under my ass. Let me get things in gear, make myself into something. She always wanted me to do that. You know what I'm saying?

RSV: [Nods head] Yeah, I know.

How do you think you overcame these obstacles? You said your grandmother inspired you. Was there anything else that helped you?

AV: The things that helped me get past being in prison were Papa, my mother, and just thinking about my grandmother.

When I was in the joint, I was just thinking about the people outside that were thinking about me every day. Those were my parents, because I could imagine if my kid was locked up, I'd be thinking about them every single day. I was really depressed. I get depressed easily because I'm a deep thinker. Sometimes it works in my favor, sometimes it works against me.

I ain't even gonna lie, I felt like killing myself a couple of times. I don't know if I felt like killing myself or if I just didn't want to live anymore, because those are two different things. Feeling suicidal is different. I don't think I ever had the courage to do it. But I still feel like that sometimes these days because life is hard.

RSV: Yeah, it is.

AV: I've been through a lot in my twenties, things that I don't think any 20-year-old should go through.

How do you view those struggles? Do you think they were worth it?

AV: I believe everything happens for a reason. I believe that some way, somehow, there's always a reason. I might not be too religious, but I am of some sort. I believe in God, but there are things I don't believe in also.

I would ask God, why did I have to go to jail? I feel like if I didn't go to jail, maybe something out on the streets might have happened to me. Maybe I needed to be in there to learn a life lesson or something.

In a way, I feel like it was still too harsh for me because I'm still messed up from it. You know, it was six months, and it scarred me for life. Not jail, but all what happened to me. I'm still dealing with it.

Even my grandmother dying is funny, because I went to jail two years after, but while my granny was sick, I was working at the hospital part-time. I was helping take care of her. I was spending a lot more time with her every day before I went to work. It was always just me and her. It was never like that before, so I felt like that prepared me for her death, because I was spending more and more time with her. I was actually watching her go through these changes, chemo and everything. For that matter, I feel like that's the reason for that.

RSV: I feel you. Even if we can't understand it at the time, everything we go through has a purpose.

What do you think your future holds for you? Where do you see yourself in five years?

AV: Owning my own business, my own restaurant. I want to build an empire, but of course that takes a lot of hard work. I see myself either in Seattle or California. Somewhere on the West Coast.

If there's a kid out there who's struggling. They're going through some tough times, like he's really messing up. What would you say to him? How would you help him get back on track based on your own experiences?

AV: They have to follow their heart. Reach inside and find your heart, because your heart is going to lead you to what you love and what you love to do. Look inside yourself.

RSV: Thanks, I really appreciate the interview.

AV: Yeah, for sure.

We Could All Use a Break

June 18th, 2015

The truth is, we all need to get away at some point. We could all use an opportunity to step back and take a breath. We need a period of time when we can detach ourselves from the grind, even if it's only for a moment.

Of course, there will be times in our lives when we cannot realistically afford such a luxury (due to the lack of time or money), which is why it's vitally important that when we can rest, we do.

Mantras like "no days off" are motivating but should be viewed appropriately. Constantly grinding at whatever it is we do, without a break, can lead us to resent what we once loved and may ultimately cause us to burn out. Rest allows us to recharge and relax our minds. By doing so, we not only come back to work refreshed, but it can provide us with new perspectives on lingering problems.

I've always taken pride in working hard at things I'm passionate about. I enjoy staying up late or waking up early in order to hone my craft. But I've learned through the years that if this habit is not managed properly, I'm doing more harm than good.

A couple of years ago, while I was in the midst of working on the manuscript for my YA novel, I would routinely find myself up 'til the wee hours of the morning, struggling to further the plot or craft dialogue.

I rarely slept. I didn't think this was a big deal because I firmly believed (and still do) that sacrifices had to be made in order to accomplish anything. However, I was ignoring the importance of rest and the effect it was having on my body.

Even though my mind was fatigued, I continued to demand that it perform at a high level. I was wearing myself out, and because of that, the ideas came slower and less frequently. This was especially worrisome due to the fact that my mind was usually home to multiple vibrant and fantastical universes playing out simultaneously.

Because of my exhaustion, the teeming metropolis that was my imagination had been reduced to an apocalyptic wasteland. If I had any hope of finishing my manuscript, I had to figure out how to repopulate my imagination.

The answer was simple: take a break. I allowed my mind to focus on the other things I enjoyed but that were not directly related to my dream. For example, I started reading comic books again. I allocated one night a month, when the new *Justice League* comic debuted, to reading and enjoying that without interruption. I let my mind soak and relish in a universe where the spectacular was ordinary.

Doing that planted fresh seeds into the soil of my imagination.

In order to regularly water these seeds, I would carve out some time before I would write to take a short nap. This allowed the seeds to take root and sprout. I then provided them with further nourishment by going once a week to see a movie or, if I couldn't afford it, find one on TV. These things brought new life to my depleted imagination. By giving my mind a break, I was able to locate the answers that eluded me.

It wasn't long before I was able to plug plot holes and complete engaging dialogue. In time, I was not only able to finish my manuscript, but I was proud of the work I had been able to produce.

I have kept this routine, and it continues to help. It helps when writing posts, searching for an agent, or revising my manuscript. Our minds and bodies are more than capable of handling rigorous workloads, but only if given time to properly recuperate. Even God rested when creating the Earth and actually demands that we do, too.

We are not admitting defeat or being weak when we decide to rest. It's quite the contrary, we are actually better preparing our bodies to handle the grind that's ahead.

Now, like all things, rest can be overdone. It's our responsibility to police ourselves. We have to be careful not to overindulge and become more focused on having fun and kicking back than getting things done. We must take enough time off so that our rest will sharpen our minds and not dull them. It's a delicate balance that we each must figure out for ourselves.

In order to optimize our abilities and eventually achieve our dreams, we have to find something that gives us peace or rest and reinvigorates our minds and bodies. It's up to us to discover what that is.

Remember:

1. Taking time off is not a bad thing.

2. However, we cannot afford to overindulge.

3. "There is virtue in work and there is virtue in rest. Use both and overlook neither."

— Alan Cohen

Run Your Race

June 25th, 2015

In 2003, I went to see the movie *Head of State*. It stars Chris Rock as an alderman who runs for President of the United States; I was about 11 years old. I'm by no means the biggest Chris Rock fan, but at the time, it was the funniest movie I had ever seen.

As the years passed, the jokes that had me doubled over in laughter faded from memory, but one piece of dialogue still rings clear in my mind as if I had heard it this morning:

"Just run your race."

This particular line was said by Tamala Jones, Rock's love interest, when she was encouraging him to focus on his campaign and ignore all outside influences. She used a great analogy of horses in a horse race. They wear blinders and are unable to see anything but what is right in front of them. With those blinders up, every bit of their attention is devoted to finishing their race.

Jones was urging Rock to concentrate only on the things he could control. If he could do that and be the best that he could possibly be, then he would shine just as brilliantly, if not more so, than his highly qualified and more accomplished opponent.

Since Rock was the star of the movie and it's Hollywood, he did win the presidency. But those facts do not detract anything from the truth of the lesson.

"Keeping up with the Joneses" is a popular idiom. It refers to our habit of comparing what we have to our peers. We tend to gauge our own success on whether or not we have accumulated as much as our neighbor. This is a dangerous game.

If we base our success solely on whether we can afford the same luxuries or obtain the same level of popularity as others, we will eventually bury ourselves under the weight of our own discontent.

We can never reach our full potential if we are always wrapped up in someone else's life. From time to time, we all fall victim to this, especially if someone we know or are close to obtains a new level of success. We begin to measure our abilities and talents against theirs. This is the fastest way to burn away confidence.

We don't all have the same amount of talent, and sometimes we long to be someone else because of what they can do. It happens. The truth is, we can't all be superstars, but that *does not* mean we can't all shine.

For the most part, we will all eventually realize that there are individuals in our fields more gifted than us, to the point where there are no equalizers. Some of us will try to compensate with our persistence and heart, but sometimes that's not enough. I don't write this in order to rain on our dreams—no, I write this so that we can all achieve them.

Everyone is on their own journey, and all we can do is run our own race. We shouldn't waste our time worrying about what someone else is doing, and we can't hurry things along because we think we deserve something that someone else has. Everything comes in due time.

We have to make do with the cards we were dealt. We have to come to grips with our limitations and embrace them. We do ourselves a disservice by basing our talent's worth on how it compares to others.

Yes, using the achievements of others as inspiration and motivation is perfectly fine, and I encourage it. But the worthiness of the work we produce cannot be based on someone else's accomplishments.

Our work stands alone, because only we can do the work that God has put us here to do. There is no need for us to feel anxious, because our time in the sun will come.

When we're comfortable with ourselves and what we bring to the table, we will find very little need in comparing ourselves to others and we will be able to appreciate our achievements for the great works that they are.

Remember:

1. God gives us enough talent to do what we were put here to do.

2. We can use the success of others as motivation, but we should not allow ourselves to be envious.

3. "Just run your race."

— Tamala Jones

200%

July 9th, 2015

I imagine most would agree that when we put forth 100% effort, we have done all that can be reasonably asked of us. And when we give 110%, we are going above and beyond. But what if that's incorrect? What if that's only a portion of what we can actually give?

To illustrate my point, I'm going to divide the mind and body into two separate entities, giving each their own 100% effort scales. Let's say we're working on a task and our body is giving 100%, but our mind is only partially engaged at 25% while the other 75% is daydreaming. Clearly, in this instance we're not giving our all, even though we may feel *physically* drained afterward. This happens to us all the time.

I've written in multiple posts about how we must lose ourselves in our passions in order to achieve the level of greatness that few ever reach. However, I never really quantified the amount of effort needed to achieve such greatness. I actually don't think I was able to articulate it properly until I saw the movie *Whiplash*.

The movie stars Miles Teller as a young jazz drummer with aspirations of greatness and J.K. Simmons as an instructor bent on pulling said greatness out of anyone who is able to endure his teaching methods.

I immediately fell in love with this movie and instantly related to Teller's character. The young artist craving to be pushed and molded into something great. He wanted nothing else but to master his craft and display his expertise to the world. Naturally, I was left with a lot to digest after the movie.

I thought at length about the interactions that occur between the body and the mind, and how we sometimes mistake our partial engagement for full engagement.

I'm sure we can all remember times when our body was present, but our mind was elsewhere. For example, I can remember basketball practices where my body ran, sweated, gave all it had, but my mind was focused on what I was going to do after.

After watching *Whiplash*, I realized that in order to reach that rare air of true greatness, we must give 200%. Meaning that when we are working on our craft, our body and mind must be perfectly in tune and functioning at their highest level. This can be difficult, which is why I recommend starting in small intervals.

There is a reason why so few people ever reach that level of greatness. It's exhausting and frightening. I believe we're afraid that if we devote too much effort to any one thing, we might snap if it doesn't pan out. But it's that point where we snap, or are on the brink of snapping, that our true genius is awakened.

When we snap or break, it is not the end but a new beginning.

To reach that point, we have to decide to give 100% of our mind and 100% of our body. Nothing less.

Our fate is in our hands. One of the most influential factors in determining our fate is the effort we put forth in creating the future in which we wish to live. And one of the few things we actually have control of in our lives is our effort.

Kobe Bryant, arguably the NBA's all-time greatest shooting guard, said it best in his *Muse* documentary:

> *"There's a choice that we have to make as people, as individuals. If you want to be great at something, there's a choice you have to make. We all can be masters at our craft, but you have to make a choice. What I mean by that is, there are inherent sacrifices that come along with that: family time, hanging out with friends, being a great friend, being a great son, nephew, whatever the case may be. There are sacrifices that come along with making that decision."*

When we give 200%, we may lose family time, free time, and even friends. Because focusing completely on one task doesn't leave much room for anything else.

Understandably, that is not a life that everyone wants, but in order to be masters of our craft, it's a road we must travel. The thing is, we can give 100% to what we do and live a good life, leaving the other 100% untapped. We won't master our craft, but we will be proficient enough to garner recognition for it and live comfortably.

Yet when we have the capacity for so much more, why leave it on the table?

Remember:

1. We have to devote 100% of our body and 100% of our mind to our craft.

2. Greatness is a choice—decide if you're willing to give 200%.

3. "We all have dreams. But in order to make dreams come into reality, it takes an awful lot of determination, dedication, self-discipline, and effort."
— Jesse Owens

Ramblings on Love – July 25th, 2014 – 1:09AM

Forever Rivals

Their rivalry will forever mesmerize me.

For example, when the eyes first catch a glimpse of Her, the heart is awakened. It stretches its legs and begins to tug on all parts of the body, it causes the hands to moisten and the stomach to flutter.

When the heart is awakened, the mind is immediately alerted of the possible danger. At first, the mind simply watches--it has always been intrigued by the heart's passion. But as things develop and the heart begins to seize complete control of the body, the mind screams in protest and orders the body to run from the situation, but by this time the mind has been overthrown.

The mind watches in horror as the heart manipulates the body and orders it to take uncalculated risks, pursue dreams, take leaps of faith, and fall madly and passionately in love.

For the mind knows all too well that it will have to mend the heart when the leap does not go as planned. It is the mind that will have to rally and take control of the body while the heart

Ramblings on Love – July 25th, 2014 – 1:09AM

mourns and begs for the mind to accompany it down memory lane to wallow in self-pity. And it is the mind that will eventually get the heart pumping again. Sadly, it is also the mind that will again watch as the heart inevitably seizes control of the body and prepares for another go-around, as always the mind's cries will go unheeded.

The mind only wants what is best for the body, and that is joy. For joy is self-sustaining and lacks the fickle nature of happiness. So as much as the mind loathes cleaning up after the heart, it will continue to do so because it knows joy will only be attained through the fulfillment of the heart's passions.

Since the mind is made up of logic and reason, it must hope in secret. So whenever the heart has control, it does just that. It secretly hopes that this time, the dream is achieved, the love is reciprocated, and the risk pays off. Even though the mind won't admit it, it needs the heart just as much as the heart needs the mind.

Their relationship will forever mesmerize me.

— R.S. Veira

Grind in Silence

July 30th, 2015

I believe there's a part in all of us that loves to boast to others about what we're doing or what we're up to. We want them to see how hard we work and know of all the sacrifices we make. This is something that a lot of us, myself included, do on social media.

I don't think there's anything particularly wrong with it, but like all things, it can be overdone. We cannot afford to invest all our attention into documenting our hard work for others and lose focus on doing the work itself.

The fact of the matter is that there are stories of our grind that we must keep to ourselves. These stories are the ones that almost sound like bragging if we were to tell them. The ones when we were up far later than we should've been, piecing together our dreams. Or the times when we went to the gym or library in the wee hours of the morning because we just had to get whatever it was done. Those stories aren't the ones we tell, but the ones others tell for us.

We have to be so focused on what we do that showing off the process to others rarely crosses our minds. We shouldn't feel the need to stage our grind so that it can be seen by spectators. We shouldn't go out of our way to show that we are working hard.

If we are truly grinding, then someone will see, most likely unbeknownst to us, and when we have accomplished our goal or achieved our dream, they will gladly tell the part of the story they witnessed. They will fill everyone in on the odd things we had to do in order to make our dreams a reality. They'll do this because everyone wants to be a part of something great.

For example, how often do we hear Michael Jordan go into great detail about how much work he put into his career? Not too often. We hear about it much more from others. Those who were present during his gradual ascent to greatness can't help but share what they witnessed.

Imagine if Jordan had never become great. We would've never heard those stories from his trainer, team executives, and random bystanders about his competitive spirit and ruthless will.

The funny thing is, the more we tell others how hard we work, the less likely they are to believe us. It's when we give up this futile pursuit of trying to show off how diligent we are that our work ethic is truly appreciated. It's then that our legacy will begin to take form.

Honestly, most people won't really care about what we do until we are successful or have achieved our dream. Unless we become the individuals that we claim one day we will be, no one wants to hear our story.

In the end, when we have reached the mountaintop and achieved our dream, our story will not only be worth reading but worth telling. And we will not be the only ones wanting to tell it.

Remember:

1. We don't need to constantly update people on how hard we work.

2. There is nothing wrong with keeping people out of the loop and grinding in silence.

Seize the Day

August 13th, 2015

A few years ago, there was a commercial for Everest College on TV. It featured a guy enthusiastically telling the audience to not only stop procrastinating but to immediately get off the couch and make the decision to better their life by enrolling at Everest. The commercial was unintentionally hilarious, and because of this it was often parodied, but the message behind the commercial was sound.

There's something about putting an errand or chore off for a later date that can be really attractive to us. On any given day, we may find ourselves to be more tired than usual or just feeling lazy, and we convince ourselves that we can do whatever it is that we have to do the following day.

Eventually, the work will get done, but what we don't think about is what could've happened if we had done the work right away. Timing is everything, and deciding not to work on our craft even for one day could push the fulfillment of our dream back weeks, months, or even years.

For example, imagine you're an artist and you have planned to put on an exhibition to display your work. You procrastinated, and days before the show, you have to rush to finish the final pieces of the exhibit. It's not your best work, but you tell yourself it's your first exhibition so it's no big deal.

The day of your exhibition arrives, and a renowned art dealer walks in because his flight was canceled; he decided to check out the local talent since he had time to spare. He stays for a while but ultimately leaves unimpressed. If you had seized the opportunity and displayed your best work, could that have been your big break?

Truthfully, who knows? Even with your best work on display, nothing may have happened. There's no way of telling, but years could go by before you're given another opportunity like that.

Of course, this is a hypothetical situation, but that's how life works. We never know who could walk into our store or pick up a magazine in which our work is featured or even stumble across our blog while surfing the web. We never know when the chance to take the next step in our career will arise, and that is why we must always put our best foot forward and be prepared.

We must believe that any day could be our day, and in order to live our dreams, we have to learn how to seize an opportunity when an opportunity presents itself.

This can be difficult at times, and sometimes I find it hard myself. While writing this post, I took periodic breaks, and during each one, I told myself that I would have more than enough time to finish the post later. It wasn't until halfway through my *third* break that I realized I had to finish this right away or it wouldn't be ready for this week.

Similarly, I'm currently going through another round of edits for my manuscript, and there are times I want to push it off for another day because editing can be really boring. Last week, in particular, there were a string of days where I spent the majority of them procrastinating until late into the night. The point is we are all susceptible to procrastination. The trick is to find a way to do what we have to despite it.

In my case, I decided to try something different to end my procrastination. I read some of the passages I had been working on aloud to a few friends who had not been in my peer review groups. This not only gave me new ideas on how to tighten it up, but their enthusiasm for the material encouraged me to *want* to do it.

Finding a way to do what we have to when we don't want to is one of the keys to fulfilling our dreams. Seize the day, because any opportunity could be *the opportunity* that changes everything.

Remember:

1. Seize the day, and take advantage of opportunities when they present themselves.

2. Share what you're working on with friends. It may provide new ideas or fresh motivation.

3. Luck favors the prepared.

Decisions, Decisions

August 20th, 2015

It's common while lying in bed at night to dissect all the decisions that brought us to this point in our lives. Right before we drift off to sleep, our minds seem to be the clearest; it's then that our brains decide it's time to replay all the choices we've ever made and play out all the possible alternate outcomes.

The truth is, we make our own decisions, and because of that, we have to take responsibility for the lives we live, good or bad. Life has an infamous reputation of being unfair, and sometimes it deals us hands that we have no chance of winning with. We can't control what we're dealt, but we can decide how we respond.

You see, it's how we handle our obstacles that determines the kind of life we will live.

It's not difficult to blame the parts of our lives where we struggled on those who wronged us or the unfair circumstances we may have found ourselves in. Maybe it was a parent who didn't support us or a friend who let us down when we needed them most. Our misfortune at that specific time in our lives may have been because of it, but the decision to allow it to affect the rest of our lives is up to us.

We can either let that pain slowly destroy us or use it to build the foundation for our future. Harboring ill feelings toward those who have wronged us or situations where we were slighted only harms us in the end. We become so focused on asking, "Why has this happened to me?" that we never actually deal with the problem in the first place. Instead of asking ourselves, "Why?" we must ask ourselves, "What's next?"

Depending on which question we ask during our times of tribulation can color how we react to things for the rest of our lives. If we continue to only ask, "Why me?" we're just throwing ourselves a never-ending pity party. The floodgates will open, and we'll overwhelm ourselves with questions like, "Why did my best friend let me down? Why did I get fired? Why does my teacher pick on me?"

The precise answers to these questions may never be figured out, because just like us, the people who have done these things to us have their own complex motivations and struggles that have led them to the decisions they made. It's impossible to figure out the reason behind everything that goes wrong in our lives. We can either waste all our time trying to figure out why, or we can decide to keep moving forward.

Back in high school, I wasn't getting much playing time during my sophomore and junior years on the varsity basketball team. I spent a lot of my time asking myself, "Why? Was I not good enough? Was it that I didn't play defense or couldn't score?" Even when I asked these questions aloud to my coach, I wasn't given any meaningful answers, and to this day I still don't know why.

So I stopped asking, "Why?" and started asking, "What's next?" I then decided that when I did get some time on the floor, I would maximize it instead of wallowing in self-pity and indignation. In the end, as I explained in previous posts, I transferred high schools in my senior year, had an amazing basketball season, and eventually, I found myself on the team at Cleveland State.

I knew the situation I was in during high school was not right for me, and because of that, I was faced with a decision. I could either allow my dream to die and forever blame my coach, and ultimately my own cowardice for allowing someone other than me to dictate my future, or I could take a leap of faith and go after my dream in spite of the pain I had experienced.

That decision has played a part in every choice I've made since. It's a core reason I moved to Los Angeles. I decided that I would never allow someone else or a situation to determine the validity of my dreams.

The success or failure of my dreams will rest solely on my shoulders.

God has blessed us with the ability to make choices. We decide how we respond to the pitfalls of life. When things go wrong we don't need to ask, "Why?" we need only ask, "What's next?"

Remember:

1. Our past pain doesn't have to ruin our future happiness.

2. We are the result of the decisions we make, so decide not to ask, "Why me?" but "What's next?"

3. "It's in your moments of decision that your destiny is shaped."

— Tony Robbins

Learning from the Greats
August 27th, 2015

Earlier this week, I was watching a couple of NBA Throwback matchups on YouTube, and I started thinking about how important it is to know the history of your industry.

First, I watched Kobe Bryant match up against Tracy McGrady in 2001, and then I watched Kobe go to war against Allen Iverson in the 2001 NBA Finals. What struck me most poignantly while watching these greats in their heyday was how easy it is to forget the past.

Understandably, we are primarily focused on the present and the events that are unfolding before us, but we must also be aware of the past. Having an appreciation for the past plays a crucial role when dealing with our future, especially when it comes to the industry we wish to enter. Learning how previous greats in our industries thought and operated provides invaluable insight into how to reach similar heights.

In an age where information is only a click away, we have no excuse for not researching the great ones before us. We should have no trouble doing that; in fact, we should enjoy it. For example, if you see yourself as an innovator, you should know of Steve Jobs, the Wright Brothers, and Walt Disney, just to name a few.

However, it's not enough to know their names. We should investigate their past. We should look for the decisions that helped shape them into the people they became. We should search for the moments where they doubted themselves and how they responded to such doubt. We should aim to find the points in their journey where they took missteps and then learn from them so we may hopefully avoid them ourselves.

They have achieved what we are ultimately aiming for, and they can provide a blueprint. No two journeys will be the same, but their journeys can give us an idea of the mindset we will need to have.

Kobe Bryant, starting shooting guard for the Los Angeles Lakers, sometimes gets flak for imitating many of Michael Jordan's moves on the court. From his step-back jumper to his fade away, there are similarities. However, why is that a problem?

He studied the greatest and learned from him. He learned how Jordan thought and saw the game. Armed with that knowledge, Kobe was able to make each one of his own moves more effective and deadly. He then brought his own swagger, flare, and signature to it. He created his own game from it. Through his appreciation and understanding of what came before, he was able to not only construct his own legacy but become one of the greatest to ever play the game.

That's a lesson we must all take to heart. In whatever it is that we do, we must identify and learn from those who were great before us.

Stephen King is one of my biggest inspirations when it comes to writing. The way he builds a world and creates a compelling atmosphere is remarkable. He is one of the greatest authors of our time, and because of that, I wanted to learn more about him. So I went searching for information on him. I learned about where he was from, and the early obstacles he faced. I even started reading his book *On Writing* to get an idea of how his mind works.

I also looked into the stories behind J.K. Rowling, Rick Riordan, and other prominent young adult authors to gain an idea of what could lie ahead.

This is all part of the process. We save ourselves countless missteps if we just take the time to learn the paths walked by those before us. We must consider this to be nearly as important as honing our own craft.

However, it's important to remember when studying these great individuals that we are not trying to *be* them, we are just trying to *learn* from them. The information we gain will help us to enhance our own skills and realize our potential.

We must learn what it takes to be great before we can be.

Remember:

1. Learn from the greats in your industry.

2. Use the lessons learned to avoid potential pitfalls and obstacles.

3. "I don't want to be the next Michael Jordan. I only want to be Kobe Bryant."

— Kobe Bryant

Ramblings on Life – November 20th, 2016 – 10:32PM

My Beliefs at 25

1. Life is a PROCESS.

2. Patience can be mind-numbingly hard BUT it's worth it every time.

3. The Big Guy (God) has a plan, always.

4. I will be great.

5. If you truly walk by faith, no experience is a bad one. It's just another one.

6. We learn the most from our pain.

7. History will repeat itself if you don't change your habits.

8. You have to accept yourself.

9. Success is how you define it, so make it a worthwhile pursuit.

10. You are where you are at that moment. Embrace it. Remember it. Move on.

— R.S. Veira

Keep Calm & Enjoy the Journey 2
September 10th, 2015

I was sitting on the beach last week, and I couldn't help but smile. Of course, that's usually what happens when one is on the beach, but this was different. The smile wasn't caused by the beauty that was before me but by the events that led to me sitting on that particular beach. The chance meetings, and the unlikely friendships that came from them, replayed over and over in my head.

Up to that point, I had only been in Los Angeles for about three weeks. I had gone from homeless to living by the beach, and that alone was something to smile about.

About a year ago, I realized that the journey to my dream was going to lead me out west. The plan started to take form last summer when I found myself on the brink of graduation and still debating on what route I should travel after I crossed that stage.

I knew I wanted to write novels and eventually screenplays, but I wasn't sure where. That was my only problem. Even though I loved Cleveland, I knew I had to leave and find my own way. So as with all life-altering decisions, I went to the Big Guy upstairs for help; I prayed for guidance and an idea of where to go. It wasn't long before the Hollywood lights were shining through my apartment window.

I began to play around with the idea of moving across the country, and the more I thought about it, the more it excited me. Leaving everything I knew behind gave me pause, but I had done it before when I transferred high schools and then colleges. I learned from those experiences that the people who want to be a part of your life will find a way, and those who don't will fade.

In order to achieve our dreams, our dreams have to be our main focus. Our dream has to direct our actions. So I decided I would leave the following summer.

As the weeks passed, I started to let those closest to me in on my plans, and to my surprise, a couple of my friends decided they wanted to come too. With a crew in tow, I began to let anyone who inquired about my plans after graduation know. It went pretty much as expected; most people smiled and nodded. They asked me why and I told them, but I always got the feeling they didn't think I would really go.

I didn't let that phase me, because I knew in a year's time I wouldn't be around and then they would know I was serious. Actions always speak louder than words.

For the next 12 months, I began working and saving money for my move. At no point in those 12 months was I at all sure how this was going to work. All I knew was that if I truly moved by faith and pursued my dream, then everything would fall into place.

The months ticked away, and before I knew it, the night before my flight had arrived. That night there were still a few details up in the air, such as where we were going to live, but I had come too far to allow any doubt to creep into my mind.

When we take a true leap of faith, by definition, we have no idea how things will work out. We have to embrace that uncertainty or it will deter us. I packed two bags full of clothes, my backpack with a few necessities, and brought a pillow so wherever I slept, I would at least have something familiar to lie on.

I slept the majority of my flight since I had spent the entirety of the previous night packing. When I landed, my cousin, who had moved to Los Angeles a month before, picked me up. He had stayed with a mutual friend for the last month, and my arrival meant it was time to find our own place.

We had been searching for an apartment for about a month before I arrived. I would set up the appointments from Cleveland, and my cousin would check them out. But nothing ever manifested. So for my first night in LA, we slept in his car, and I had never been so happy. I went to sleep with a smile on my face.

Sleeping in his car was our plan for the first week while our housing situation solidified, but God had other plans.

During the second night, while we were looking for a place to park and sleep, we were invited by a friend to crash at his apartment for a few days. He had a spacious place in Marina del Rey. The lease was about to be up and everyone was moving out, so us staying there wasn't a big deal.

A few days turned into a week, and by the end of the week, one of the roommates who didn't want to move offered us a spot on the lease. The next thing I knew, after a few more small miracles, it was our apartment, and we were living by the beach.

The thing about the journey and taking the road less traveled is that no matter how much we prepare, we will never be ready for the twists and turns that are ahead of us. That can strike true fear into our hearts and force us to never leave the beaten path, but if we can muster the courage to move by faith and refuse to have our actions dictated by fear, there is absolutely nothing that cannot be achieved. It's possible; I'm living proof.

There's a remarkable journey that lies ahead of each of us, but it's only for those who are willing to leave the ready-made road and travel through the thicket, forging their own path.

Remember:

1. Have faith and follow your dream, even if it leads you to new or distant places.

2. Enjoy the uncertainty of the journey; embrace it.

3. "Two roads diverged in a wood, and I took the one less traveled by, and that has made all the difference."

— Robert Frost

Is the Juice Worth the Squeeze?

September 17th, 2015

One of my favorite movie quotes comes from *The Girl Next Door*. During the main character's wacky adventure to date his new neighbor, filled with increasingly difficult obstacles, he is asked a very reasonable question: "Is the juice worth the squeeze?" Which basically means is the effort that is being put forth worthwhile? I think it's a question we all ask ourselves in some form at some point.

When we are pursuing anything, the obstacles that must be overcome and the time that must be invested to be successful can sometimes cause us to question if what we're working toward is even worth the effort.

In order to figure out if the time and effort we invest is worthwhile, we have to have a clear idea of the end goal, and the end goal must be important to us. It doesn't have to mean anything to anyone else. You see, it's very likely that we spend our energy on things that in our minds are worthwhile, but in the eyes of others are a waste of time.

Naturally, this relates directly to our dreams.

At the end of the day, how we use our time is determined by what we believe is important. That is a fact. So when we invest large quantities of time into whatever activities we do, we have to ensure it's something *we* value.

During the summer after my freshman year of college, I would go to the gym four days a week, walking a mile and a half to the gym to lift and a mile and a half home. There was a practical reason behind this: my parents worked and couldn't take me every time I needed to go. So I decided to cut out the middleman and just walk.

The whole ordeal would take about three and a half to four hours. I then spent the rest of my time working so that I could afford the gym membership, and the time I had leftover I spent shooting in the gym. I believed this was a useful way to spend my time because I was pursuing my dream of playing college basketball.

I was consistently asked why I was doing all this. Some thought my time would be better spent getting an internship, and others believed I should just enjoy my first college summer. But I knew the juice would be worth the squeeze, and it was.

That summer instilled in me that when given enough time, walking is always a viable option. This lesson has been especially invaluable since I currently don't have a car and don't want to pay for a Lyft or Uber unless absolutely necessary. I've embraced walking and taking the bus and use them as an opportunity to better acquaint myself with Los Angeles.

I wholeheartedly believe that if we conclude the juice is worth the squeeze in any endeavor we find ourselves caught up in, as we march toward our dreams, it will turn out to be worthwhile; either immediately or down the road.

Remember:

1. "Is the juice worth the squeeze?"

— *The Girl Next Door*

What a Time to Chase a Dream

September 24th, 2015

I love an underdog story. I find a story about someone who defies the odds and rises to prominence nearly irresistible. So while I was sitting on my couch last Sunday waiting for the new Drake and Future mixtape, *What a Time to be Alive*, to drop, I had to laugh.

What I found so irresistibly funny was that Drake was now at a level where his mixtape owned the attention of the majority of the internet. This is the same Drake that four to five years ago was considered too "soft." The same Drake that many critics gladly stated lacked the street cred to ever stomp with the heavyweights of the rap game, but here we were.

From where he began—an actor on a Canadian teen drama—it was ridiculous to think that one day his every move would have a major influence on the music industry and pop culture in general. His journey forces us to consider the terrifying thought of what is actually possible if our "why?" is bigger than our obstacles.

During the final minutes leading up to the mixtape's release, I wondered what motivated Drake to keep going. What was his "why?" Why did he feel it necessary to endure the public criticism and the personal shots over all these years?

I've tackled similar questions to varying degrees over the last nine months of blogging, but I never answered the most basic question, "Why?" Why do some people find it necessary to take what is in their minds and bring it into reality? Why does that become their sole focus?

I think the reason for my reluctance to address "why?" is because I've struggled to put into words exactly why I do what I do. When asked, I frequently say my "why?" is to fulfill God's purpose for my life. And that is true, but that raises another question: why do I feel the *need* to do *that*?

We can't begin to grasp the answers to such questions until we wrestle with our most basic self. This part of us is the untamed passion that roars in the pit of our soul. There comes a day when we either lock it away or set it loose. Our decision on the matter will echo throughout the rest of our lives.

I believe that when we allow ourselves to probe the parts of our minds and souls we rarely peek into, we see that there is a gaping hole we would rather ignore than face. This is where the answer to our "why?" belongs.

When we try to fill that hole with answers that center on how others will feel about our decisions, how much money we'll make, or the glorification of ourselves, we never seem to be able to fill it up. They work momentarily, at best, but never last.

When I discovered my "why?" it was in a moment of pure self-examination. I peeled back the layers of fear and uncertainty and allowed myself to see myself in my rawest form. My three passions—writing, basketball, and inspiring others—were bare before me. In one hand, I held a key to both their imprisonment and freedom.

The option to lock them up and pursue a more traditional route was tempting, because I knew from basketball that if I let them free, I would be forced to go places and do things that at first would be terribly frightening. I would be forced to challenge myself and battle self-doubt on a daily basis. I would be forced to deal with public doubt and criticism when I bared my heart and mind every week on this blog.

But when I weighed all that against the joy and fulfillment that came when I engaged in each one of those activities, the negatives were negligible. I finally understood my "why?" I reasoned that those three things had been at my center since the day God breathed life into my lungs. It was just up to me to identify them. Once I did that, it was clear I would be dead wrong to pursue anything else. Anything else would be a waste of my time.

My "why?"—the full realization of the gifts God has given me—is far bigger than me, and it has to be. We are not living just for ourselves but for everyone we come in contact with, directly or indirectly.

If I had never watched Degrassi growing up and witnessed Drake evolve from teen actor to one of the most successful musicians of my generation, would I still believe that anything is possible? Who knows? How many countless others has he influenced the same way?

As dreamers, our collective "why?" is not only to live out our dreams but to liberate the imaginations and minds of those who don't even know they're imprisoned.

We live in a time where a biracial, Canadian, Jewish rapper who candidly expresses himself in his art is currently one of the most influential people in the music industry. What a time to be alive, indeed, and more importantly, what a time to chase a dream.

Remember:

1. Why do you do what you do?

2. When you deny your why and turn your back to your passions, you not only kill your dreams but the dreams of the people you would have inspired.

3. "And as we let our own light shine, we unconsciously give others permission to do the same. As we are liberated from our own fear, our presence automatically liberates others."
   — Marianne Williamson

Crunch Time

October 1st, 2015

Pressure is something we all face and handle differently. Some of us bend, break, or thrive under its weight. If we can learn to embrace and operate under pressure, we take another step closer to living our dreams. Make no mistake, in order to reach the pinnacle of our potential, we have to be able to remain calm when the stakes are the highest.

Like all things, there are those of us who are naturally better under pressure than others. However, this should not discourage us, because dealing with pressure is something I believe can be learned.

It's safe to say that in order to be the best, we need pressure. Nature provides an excellent example of this. Pressure helps form one of the most precious and sought-after jewels in the world. About 100 miles below the Earth's surface, a combination of intense heat and pressure is used to create diamonds. Therefore, it's only logical that pressure is needed in order for us to shine like diamonds.

We admire those who handle pressure well, and rightly so.

High-pressure situations have always been able to capture the imagination. We're at the edge of our seats in the movie theater when the hero has only seconds to decide which wire to cut before a bomb goes off and levels the city. This also applies to sports. A key criterion in measuring the greatness of our sports icons is how well they handle themselves during crunch time.

When it's all on the line, are they able to produce?

That question also applies to all of us, in all disciplines. For example, we could be tasked with brokering a major deal for our firm, or we have to ace a final that determines if we pass a class. Pressure is all around us, and shying away from it will not help us grow. It will only help us to buckle when it is our time to step up.

In basketball, a common drill to simulate pressure is to have the team line up on the baseline, and one by one, each member has to take a free throw. If a player misses, the entire team runs the length of the court and back. If the free throw is made, then no one runs and the next person in line is up. This drill is most effective near the end of practice when everyone is winded.

Your body is fatigued, but you must keep your mind sharp. All eyes are on you when you step to the line. If you miss, the whole team runs because of you. Your legs are heavy, and your teammates are hoping you come through so they can catch their breath instead of having to sprint on tired legs. The pressure is on, and I've missed my share of free throws in that situation.

In the larger scheme of things, those stakes aren't really that high. But nonetheless, it's extremely disappointing to succumb to the pressure, and when it happens, we have to decide if we will avoid it from then on or perform in spite of it. Even though I'd missed multiple times in crunch time, I was never going to stop shooting. That and similar drills like it helped mold me into a person who is willing to take on pressure whenever it presents itself.

The first official game-winning free throws I hit were during my freshman year of high school. I can't remember the team we played, but I remember how I felt and the lesson I learned.

I remember stepping up to the line and being surprised. My mind was not racing, my breathing was calm, and my focus was unwavering. After two flicks of my wrist, the game was ours. When the buzzer sounded, it cemented the idea in my mind that training under pressure is the only way to handle pressure.

Training under pressure is something we have to be willing to do. If we always demand a certain level of excellence from ourselves, we can apply a healthy dose of pressure at all times. Not so much to burn ourselves out, but enough to keep a fire under our butts. Yes, it's unpleasant, it's nerve-racking, and it may even cause us to lose sleep. Yet despite these things, pressure is a valued ally.

Like failure, pressure gets a bad rap because it's painful and easier to avoid than to deal with head-on. And just like failure, if we don't figure out how to work with it, to learn from it, and to thrive despite it, we will never see the fulfillment of our dreams.

A diamond is formed under intense heat and pressure. Our dreams are no different.

Remember:

1. Pressure, like failure, is to be embraced, not avoided.

2. We should hold ourselves to a higher standard, which will provide us with a healthy dose of pressure at all times.

3. "When we long for life without difficulties, remind us that oaks grow strong in contrary winds and diamonds are made under pressure."
— Peter Marshall

Here & Now

October 15th, 2015

We rarely focus on the here and now. Even when our minds are at ease and we're just hanging out, we're usually too preoccupied thinking about the past or contemplating the future to focus on the present moment. It's only every once in a while that we actually find ourselves enjoying the present.

I didn't even realize I was doing this until I found myself in the midst of a really interesting conversation at the gym last week.

During this conversation, I was challenged to think of a time when I was solely focused on the now. Initially, I thought the answer was simple: all the time. However, it wasn't long before I realized that I'm actually always thinking about my next step, and that was the point.

The individual I was talking to explained to me that we are so easily caught up by the possibilities of the future or the failures of the past that the current moment is lost on us. It gets to the point where we enjoy our experiences more through memories than we do living the actual event.

But is that a bad thing? Can we really be mad at ourselves for wanting to prepare for the future? Or dissecting the past in hope of not reliving it?

I struggled with these questions over the last week. Preparing for the future is a necessity for me. Having a specific goal in mind and designing countless contingency plans to ensure I stay on task is one of my favorite pastimes. But at the same time, I was forced to consider if focusing so much on my future caused me to miss out on my present.

The truth of the matter was that to some extent, I *was* missing out on the now. Ironically, earlier in the day before my conversation in the gym, I was having a discussion with a friend about my plans after my current lease was up.

The problem was I had *just* moved in a month ago, and it's a *year* lease. It's impossible to be in two places at once, and my mind was 11 months in the future.

It would be a different story if this was the first time this has happened, but when I sat down and seriously thought about my life to that point, I have regularly been looking to the future and thinking about how great things will be when I finally get there.

However, at the same time, I'm also engaging in conversations with friends discussing how great things used to be in the "good ol' days" and how great it would be if those days had lasted longer.

This kind of thinking leads to a consistent state of unrest. We're always falling between the future and the past, and for only a few moments we find ourselves conscious in the moment.

There is nothing wrong with planning ahead or learning from the past, but we have to understand that if our minds are constantly someplace else, we are never here. If we condition our minds to operate this way, then no matter how successful we become, we will always be aiming for the "next step" in order to find fulfillment.

What I've started to do in order to break this habit is to make a conscious effort to focus on the now whenever possible. This means after I've done all I can do when it comes to planning out my future, I leave the rest in God's hands and focus on the present.

The only thing in the future we can control is the effort we put in during the present to make it a reality. In other words, the majority of the things we worry about in the future we have no control over.

When it comes to the past, we have to come to terms with the demons that live there. We all have them, they deeply influence our decisions and the way we see ourselves. The thing with the past is that it's *over* and we'll never get those moments back. Let those things go, and free yourself from those demons. The more time we dwell on them, the more time we take away from enjoying our current blessings.

It's okay to think of the future and remember the past, but when it's overdone, we lose out on the here and now. When it's overdone, we chase after a future that we never seem to reach and are stuck in a past we can't change.

Remember:

1. Enjoy the present.

2. It's fine to think and plan for the future, but don't let it consume you to the point where you're no longer present in the now.

3. "Yesterday is gone. Tomorrow has not yet come. We have only today. Let us begin."
 — Mother Teresa

Ramblings on God – August 22nd, 2020 – 3:03AM

I was sitting by the water last week when I suddenly thought, "I've lived 28 years, I have a pretty good sample size." At some point in your life, you have to take stock of the seeds you've sown and the harvests you've reaped and decide what you want to continue to plant. I will no longer plant seeds of doubt, envy, pride, lust, jealousy, malice, fear, nor selfish ambition. I will continue to plant seeds of love, joy, peace, patience, kindness, gentleness, self-control, goodness, faithfulness, and selflessness. But it's hard not to drop a few of the undesirable seeds along the way.

For example, earlier this week, I allowed myself to drink to excess and I fell back into my pride and ego, which in turn led to a bit of spiritual backsliding culminating in tonight's search to appease the flesh. I literally went out tonight solely looking to hook up with someone for no other reason than just to do it, and I'm glad God didn't allow that to happen. I'm tired of living like that and no longer find it satisfying.

There's nothing wrong or bad with anything in and of itself, but we can very easily transform the things we like/love into idols, and it's in this creation of a new god that we find a whole new level of suffering. Anything that separates us from God will ultimately leave us not only unfulfilled but lonely, afraid, and resentful in the end. This I have come to believe as fact.

So with this in mind, I shine a spotlight on all the pursuits of my life to see if they are indeed in line with God's will for my life. I think God's will for us is laid out clearly in 1 Thessalonians 5:16-18 and Micah 6:8. These verses do not say anything about seeking the honor and praise of man, and they do not say achieve your dreams. They instead say be joyful and walk humbly with your God, for that is God's will. Naturally, my next question was, "What does humility get you?" This, too, God answers. In Proverbs 22:4 it's written, "Humility and the fear of the Lord bring wealth and honor and life." God continually speaks of the riches of a life centered on Him. In Proverbs 21:21, it's written, "Whoever pursues righteousness and love finds life, prosperity, and honor." These are all the things I've been looking for.

So it seems that unless I humble myself enough to say that I don't know what will ultimately bring me fulfillment, and decide to walk humbly with my Lord in utter dependency and total reverence, then I'll never find true fulfillment.

Thankfully, God has brought me to the point where I am willing to do this. He has shown me fleshly pursuits are meaningless without Him. I have had successes, no matter how big or small they may seem to anyone else. I have had victories and relished in their spoils. Yet in the entire process of grinding, sowing, performing, and reaping, I found nothing but temporary pleasure. Yet in the midst of a global pandemic, when all my plans were put on hold, plans which when fulfilled were supposed to grant me peace, I found peace elsewhere. Peace completely outside of achievement and rooted solely in contemplating God.

It's as if everything that I constructed to provide me with happiness was in reality creating a great unhappiness in me. When contemplating God, I have recently gone hours in utter bliss, until I allow myself to ride a train of thoughts that do nothing but separate me from God and cause me pain; disguised as "self-reflection." I now see why we must be careful not to become too wrapped up in the story of ourselves.

This has been a string of loosely connected thoughts. I just needed to put them down somewhere.

Have faith, my friend, I love you.

— R.S. Veira

The Person in the Mirror

October 22nd, 2015

We've all heard the saying that we are our own worst enemy. It's no exaggeration. More times than not, we are solely responsible for the failure of our dreams. For whatever reason, we somehow manage to stand in our own way and impede our progress.

Over the last year, I've come to appreciate this idea more and more. It's a strange feeling to wake up every morning and see in the mirror the person who is holding you back. I don't believe we intentionally mean to self-sabotage ourselves, but certain factors lead us to do just that.

For example, these factors can originate from fear or self-doubt. The scariest situation we face on our journey is not failure, but taking a step forward into the unknown. We are constantly at war with ourselves. The war, for the most part, is a private one held in our minds.

Imagine our minds as a battlefield dominated by three sides. On one side, we have the person we wish to be, on another we have the person we used to be, and on the final side is the person we are. Each side is trying to lay claim to our mind, and each feels that they have the rightful claim. This war rages constantly, and our actions are the determining factor in which side is victorious.

When we fret over decisions or mistakes that we made years ago, we give fuel to the side that represents our past. If we continue to be defined by our failures, then we'll never move past them, and we ultimately become a person who lives through their past accomplishments or who never overcame their past pain. This causes us to fear change. We become attached to those moments we can never get back, and we stop all progress.

When we struggle to pull the trigger on the next stage of life, we give the edge to who we are right now. This causes us to never grow. We settle, not only because we are scared of failure but of our potential success. What if we become everything we dreamed? Could we handle it? When we actually take the time to consider what comes along with the fulfillment of our dreams, it's enough to give anyone pause.

We will no longer be "under the radar" dreamers, but instead we'll be the "poster child" of achieving the dream. It will be our responsibility to help lead others in doing the same. We'll be in the spotlight; higher expectations will be set for us from then on. The pressure to reach those expectations will not only be applied by ourselves but by those who will now profit off of our success.

There will also be repercussions if we fail to meet those standards that are set for us. Not only will our well-being be in jeopardy, but also the well-being of everyone who has come to depend on us because of what we have achieved. The fear of success is just as potent as failure. That is why for many of us, the battle for our minds is won by either the past or present.

To fulfill our dreams, we can't align with either of those two sides. It's the future, the person we wish to be, that we have to believe in wholeheartedly. We have to envision the person we will be five to 10 years down the road in order to ever make that a reality. It's similar to how I explained that it's important to write down what we want to be in order to make it *feel* more real. We have to believe that the person we are aiming to be is plausible. This will help remove the fear of taking that step into the unknown and leaving your present self behind.

This ties directly into last week's post, where I tried to point out the importance of being present in the here and now. We must be present, but we must not give in to our present self's fear of growth. In order to become the person we envision ourselves being, we have to be courageously active in the moment and handle what we can control.

I found myself dragging my feet lately, and I had no idea why. In all honesty, I was avoiding the truth. The fact of the matter was I was afraid of where everything was heading. Things were coming together and falling into place just as I had imagined. And for a brief period of time, I had cold feet about moving forward.

My past and present selves had gained the upper hand in the war of my mind, and the person I aimed to be had lost footing. It wasn't until it occurred to me that I had only come this far by my faith and my belief in God that I realized I could only go further by the same means.

My belief that a higher power is guiding my steps helped me to again throw my support fully behind the person I hope to be and thus helped steady my mind, for now.

When we stare in the mirror at ourselves in the morning, there are three possible people who can be staring back. If we are serious about living our dreams, then our reflection will be of the person we aim to be.

Remember:

1. Our mind is a war zone, and our future depends on which side we give support.

2. Fight to be the person you wish to be, not the person you are or were.

Learning from the Greats 2

October 29th, 2015

This week was the beginning of the NBA season. A time of excitement and promise, but unfortunately I lacked my usual enthusiasm. On the eve of this NBA season, I realized things would never be the same. I grew up in Cleveland, Ohio, but my favorite player is from Philadelphia. He grew up in Italy and plays basketball on the West Coast for the Los Angeles Lakers. This NBA season marks the start of Kobe Bryant's 20th season in the league and the end of one of the greatest careers in the history of the sport.

As children, it's common for us to idolize and make heroes out of our sports stars, and when their careers wind down, we are forced to say farewell. But if we chose correctly, during their playing days they showed us the importance of hard work, perseverance, and determination. They helped us believe that our dreams are possible, but only if we never fold under the ever-growing pressures to conform to the ideas others have for us and hold fast to the belief that we are not crazy to think the way we do. When their careers come to an end, we say thank you for the memories and the unforgettable lessons.

Since I was a kid, I've been driven by my passions. I've always strived to be the best I could be at whatever I did. It's only right, then, that my hero growing up was driven by a similar passion. I didn't start playing basketball seriously until fifth grade, and the first player I learned about wasn't Michael Jordan or Magic Johnson, but Kobe Bean Bryant of the Los Angeles Lakers.

From studying his early years, I learned the ins and outs of basketball. In order to get a better idea of who he was, I dove into researching his career, which at that time was only about five or six years old. I quickly learned that after he was drafted in 1996, Bryant made it clear to all that his sole goal was to be the greatest.

Byron Scott, his former teammate and current coach, said the following when reminiscing on his first interaction with an 18-year-old Bryant.

"I asked him, 'What do you want to be in this league?' And he said, 'I want to be one of the greatest of all time.'"

One of the earliest lessons I believe we all learn is that many can talk a good game, but few are actually about what they preach. In the fifth grade, I knew Kobe had won a couple of championships and was well on his way to fulfilling his dream. However, he was also playing alongside a future Hall of Famer in Shaquille O'Neal. So I had to figure out if Kobe was just a product of his situation or if his will to be the best was legitimate. I found both to be true.

On May 12th, 1997, in the Western Conference semi-finals against the Utah Jazz, a rookie Kobe Bryant shot four air balls in the course of the final moments of the game, costing the Lakers the win. This was the first defining moment of his career. When looking back at the game years later, Byron Scott put it this way:

> *"You either grow up big time like he did or you don't. There is no in-between as far as I'm concerned."*

How many of us, after a major failure or setback, never try again? As an 18-year-old, Kobe not only lost his team a playoff game, but ultimately the series because he missed the big shot not just once, but *four times*. That's enough to crush anyone's confidence. But legends and heroes aren't created by accident. It takes deliberate action and a willingness to accept nothing less than success. Bryant locked himself in the gym the following summer and emerged the next season as one of the best young players in the league.

He became the youngest NBA All-Star of all time at 19 years and 170 days old. He averaged 15.4 points on a team that won 61 games and lost only 21 that season.

Those four shots are a distant memory, as he is now considered one of the most clutch players of all time. That defeat in 1997, and his response to it, catapulted him closer to his ultimate dream of being the greatest. And depending on who you ask, he achieved his dream.

He scored over 32,400 points, passing Michael Jordan on the NBA all-time scoring list. He is the first player in NBA history to have over 30,000 points and 6,000 assists. He won five NBA championships. He is a 17-time NBA All-Star. The accolades go on and on. However, the most important accolade is that he inspired a generation of kids to defy the expectations society had placed on us.

This post could go on for another 20 to 30 pages examining his career at every turn, and then another 10 to 15 explaining how it impacted my life. I spent the majority of my middle school and high school years debating Kobe's supremacy in a town where LeBron James reigns unchallenged. However, that is not the point of this post. The point is not to argue his greatness in terms of basketball but to recognize the role he played in the life of a kid with a dream from Cleveland, Ohio.

The point is to recognize a legend who helped shape my mindset when it comes to giving it all to your passions and leaving nothing on the court or playing field of life. Truly, we can be whatever we want to be, but only if we go confidently down the path that God has set for us, and that confidence will topple any obstacles we face.

On more than one occasion, I have found myself on my last legs in a workout or suffering from an intense case of writer's block, and in those moments I think of how Kobe responded to struggles, doubters, and critics. I think of when he dragged a team with no business of even *thinking* of the post-season to the playoffs in 2006. I remember when people claimed he couldn't win without Shaq, and he then delivered two more championships to LA. I contemplate when his Achilles gave out and the critics stated his career was over, but he came back the following year and led the NBA in scoring before succumbing to a shoulder injury.

I remember these things and continue to push onward.

Thank you, Kobe, for an amazing 20 years. And hopefully one or two more.

Remember:

1. When we fail, we don't give up, but we refocus our efforts and try again.

2. Settle for nothing less than success.

3. "There's a choice that we have to make as people, as individuals. If you want to be great at something, there's a choice you have to make. We all can be masters at our craft, but you have to make a choice. What I mean by that is, there are inherent sacrifices that come along with that. Family time, hanging out with friends, being a great friend, being a great son, nephew, whatever the case may be. There are sacrifices that come along with making that decision."

— Kobe Bryant

2015: A Year in Review
November 12th, 2015

This week, I renewed my domain name and hosting package for my blog, and while in the middle of that process I naturally thought of the year that had passed.

It's been an amazing year, but like anything, there were ups and downs. There were times when I wasn't sure if I would be able to continue to post regularly, but I never missed a week. It was a combination of the encouragement I received from my readers, God, and my belief in the dream that kept me going. It was a great year, but I want next year to be even better. In order to accomplish this, I plan on providing even greater content for my readers.

It's always good to change things up. We tend to fall into routines that work well for a while but cause us to grow complacent. In order to live our dreams, we have to stay on our toes. We have to be comfortable being uncomfortable. We have to be willing to adapt and change. This idea has weighed heavily on my mind lately.

Last November, I decided it was time to branch out in a new direction in order to help build my audience and get closer to my dream of being a novelist. Even though I had purchased the domain name and hosting package, I didn't actually publish my first official post until January 16th of this year. It took me from November 'til then to figure out what I even wanted to talk about and how I was going to design the site.

After a year, I have to say that writing this blog was a great move. It was a blessing. I've been able to touch people through my writing, better my craft, and begin to build an audience. That's everything I sought to do with my blog to begin with.

Now with a new year ahead, I have a few changes that I will be trying out.

My original vision for my blog was a combination of short stories and weekly motivational posts, but that's not how it began. On January 16th, I decided to only write motivational posts about common obstacles we all face while on the journey of chasing our dreams. It wasn't until about a month in that I was encouraged by my older sister to publish a short story since writing fiction is my true passion.

It made perfect sense that I would post short fiction and/or fantasy on my blog. That's my novel's genre, and after all, the purpose of this site is to help get it published. In hindsight, it's funny that I was hesitant to share my short stories. I had been writing about taking chances and giving everything to our dreams, but *I* was holding back.

My first short story was *1428 Turner Street: Agent Jericho*. It was my most popular post at the time, reaching over 100 "likes"—these can be seen at the bottom of each post. The *Turner Street Series*, on average, quickly became my most popular posts; I also enjoyed writing them the most. Because of this, I've decided to change up my posting format.

I've decided to write a short story every other week instead of monthly. This means that two weeks of the month will be motivational posts about the Journey, and the other two weeks will be short stories. I plan on testing out the new format for the remainder of the calendar year and into 2016.

I encourage everyone who reads my blog to either provide feedback as a comment on this post or reach out to me via email (rsv@rsveira.com) about the posting changes. I would love to hear from my readers.

Thanks for a great first year, this is only the beginning.

A Couple of Highlights from the Year:

1. *A Growing Audience*: Over 1,600 likes on Facebook fan page.

2. *Bettering the Craft*: The feedback I received has helped me sharpen my writing and has provided the encouragement needed to keep pressing on.

3. *A Way to Provide Inspiration*: It's been a true blessing to be able to impact people every Thursday, be it through a

2015: A Year in Review

motivational word or providing a doorway to escape the day-to-day grind with the *Turner Street* stories.

A Day of Thanks

November 26th, 2015

Happy Thanksgiving! It's officially the holiday season, and it's time for us to give thanks for everything in our lives. When we're asked the requisite question, "What are you thankful for?" our minds usually jump to the great things that are happening to us. There's nothing wrong with this, but we should also be thankful for the times that made us uncomfortable and forced us to grow.

Every once in a while, I like to just push play on my iPad and put my music on shuffle. No matter the song that comes up, I don't change it. This allows me to hear songs that I never willingly choose and helps me uncover lost gems. Last week I was doing just that, and the audio to one of my favorite YouTube videos began to play.

The name of the video is "How Bad Do You Want It? (Success)" It's a montage of a football player honing his craft by lifting, running routes, and working on his footwork. However, the punch is provided by a voiceover done by motivational speaker Eric Thomas. I first watched this video during a period of great change in my life, and hearing it now allowed me to travel back to that time.

This video revolutionized my mindset, and it's littered with quotes that I still recite to myself today. However, I will only focus on two in this post.

> *"When you want to succeed as bad as you want to breathe, then you'll be successful."*

When I first saw that video, I was preparing to walk-on to the Xavier basketball team. It was the beginning of my sophomore year, and tryouts were around the corner. In order to stay sharp, I would wake up in the morning, head to the gym, and work out before class. When I came back to my dorm, I iced my ankle, which I badly sprained two summers before, and watched that video.

In the video, Eric Thomas tells a story about a young man who seeks the advice of a successful guru. The guru tells the young man to meet him on the beach in the morning. The young man shows up the next morning, and the guru then tells him to follow him out into the water. The young man is hesitant at first but reasons that since the guru is very successful, he should just follow along.

They walk until the water is at their mouths, and the young man stops. The young man begins to turn back, but the guru stops him and tells him that if he really wants to be successful, he must come out a little bit farther.

The young man does, and the guru immediately dunks the young man's head underwater. Right before the young man is about to pass out, the guru pulls him up and says, "When you want to succeed as bad as you want to breathe, then you'll be successful."

This anecdote resonated with my soul. I understood that mindset. I put in the work to make the Dean's List my freshman year. I then dedicated my summer to working out and getting ready for the opportunity to walk-on. There was nothing I wanted more. I had one sole focus.

Understandably, I was devastated when I didn't make the team, and it was the following quote that helped me recover.

> *"Don't cry to quit! You're already in pain, you're already hurt, get a reward from it!"*

I was lost when I didn't make that team. That's the best way to describe the all-encompassing despair. It was one of the lowest points in my life. I gave everything in preparation for it. I wholeheartedly believed I deserved it, and for a while, I was content in wallowing in my own self-pity. However, it was the quote above that helped resurrect my spirit.

I had come too far to just quit. Yes, I was hurting, but I had promised myself I was going to play Division I basketball. At the end of the semester, I packed my things up and I transferred to Cleveland State. Even though I faced my share of challenges there, I had an unbelievable two and a half years fulfilling my dream of playing Division I ball.

On this day of thanks, I am thankful for that pain.

A Day of Thanks

I am thankful for those obstacles because without them, I wouldn't be writing this post. I wouldn't be chasing my dream of being a novelist. During the times that our struggles are the greatest, we must remember that God is preparing us for what he has in store for us. If we achieve our dreams before we are either mentally, physically, emotionally, or spiritually prepared for them, we won't be able to sustain them.

Today, while we give thanks for everything that is great in our lives, remember to acknowledge the unpleasant events that preceded them, because without one, we can't have the other.

Remember:

1. Be thankful for both the pleasant and unpleasant situations God sends our way.

2. Our struggles prepare us for our eventual success.

Blueprint for Success

December 10th, 2015

Cities aren't built on a whim. There's an intricate blueprint and infrastructure that must be adhered to in order to make them a reality. Without a blueprint, we would construct roads that lead to dead ends and erect disjointed and unstable buildings. Our dreams are similar. If we don't know what we're building toward, we'll never get there.

The easiest way to begin constructing the blueprint for our dreams is to capture our ideas. Ideas, by nature, are elusive. However, if we write them down, we not only catch them but give ourselves a chance to watch them grow and evolve over time.

For me, it all started in the spring of 2012. I began drawing up my blueprint in my composition book. Looking at it now, three years later, it's awe-inspiring to see how my ideas morphed and eventually came to fruition.

The idea to write my novel came to me in late 2011/early 2012. I got my composition book during the spring of 2012, and I started playing with plot outlines. My scribbles detailed the lives of the characters, the geography of the world they would inhabit, and even the exports and imports of each nation.

As I continued to flip through the pages and 2012 gave way to 2013, I witnessed my outlines become more precise. Characters were given names, and sample dialogue was written. Ideas from the year before that didn't fit my new vision were crossed out, and ones more in line replaced them.

By the time 2013 faded and 2014 emerged, my first draft of my manuscript was finished. The chicken-scratch that filled the pages of my composition book now shifted gears. It detailed my search for an agent and my eventual decision to create this blog.

I've talked about writing down our dreams and goals before, and actually seeing my own written down reinforced my belief that it is a fundamental step in achieving our dreams. Through our blueprints, we can easily trace not only our progress but how our mindset throughout the years matured. And if we stick with our dreams long enough, we'll see things we once wrote down come to life before our eyes.

This was especially poignant when I stumbled upon the pages outlining my blog. My blueprint listed potential topics and all the possible domain names. Flipping through those pages reminded me of how everything takes time; all these posts were once unrefined ideas. Rome was not built in a day. A cliché, yes, but appropriate.

Even my search for representation was documented in my blueprint. Each agent that I queried when I first finished my manuscript, before I realized how many edits and reviews were needed, was written down in my notebook. I wrote down each one who rejected it, to use as motivation later.

After these initial rejections, and after a couple of rounds of edits and reviews, I sent out another batch of query letters. It took over 40 agent queries before I was asked to send my full manuscript.

They didn't pick it up, but I hadn't fully expected them to. I just wanted to know that my writing was improving, and it was. That's what creating a blueprint for our dreams does for us. It shows us that we are getting closer. It gives us an opportunity to watch our journey unfold. We can see how little we knew when we thought we had everything figured out. It shows us how we made adjustments when things didn't work and how our ideas were tweaked over time.

With a blueprint, we are able to not only find inspiration from our past but plot our future. One of my favorite sayings is, "When man plans, God laughs." Our blueprints can't dictate where we will end up, but they give us something to strive toward. By moving confidently in one direction, we are destined to eventually get to where we want to go.

Remember:

1. Invest in a notebook or journal and plot out your plans for the future.

2. Our blueprints aren't the end-all solution. Be open to

changes, because that's life, but keep moving toward your ultimate goal.

3. "Everybody that's successful lays out a blueprint."

— Kevin Hart

Ramblings on God – November 23rd, 2020 – 11:57PM

About six years ago, I began laying the foundation for R.S. Veira, so to see that we now have a Google Knowledge Panel is amazing. I don't even know how to set those things up. One day, it was just there. A true act of God. It is the perfect example of God working all the time, and mostly in ways unbeknownst to me until the appointed time. God truly orchestrates and does everything, I just show up. It's a wonderful partnership.

I have laid everything at His feet, and I now know that it will all play out exactly how it needs to, and I can rejoice in that knowledge. Everything God has or will put me through has been or will be for my ultimate good. We set out to be a basketball player, and we became one. We set out to become a storyteller, and we became one. I am a child of the Most High God, and with my God, we can be and do anything. Thank you for not giving up on me, Lord.

Have faith, my friend, I love you.

— R.S. Veira

A Good Poker Face

January 14th, 2016

Imagine you wake up and your house is on fire. While stumbling through the smoke-filled rooms in your haste to get out, you stub your toe on the corner of a chair you didn't see due to the aforementioned smoke. Your lungs burn and your vision is blurry. However, the front door is in sight, but you suddenly remember you have to get your dog. Sadly, you don't have to look long. You see your dog motionless on the floor. He passed away due to smoke inhalation. When you finally get out of your home and are standing on your front lawn, you remember that the day before, you pulled out your entire savings because you didn't trust the banking system and hid the money under your mattress. The mattress you left in your burning house.

This is how life feels sometimes.

There are times it seems like everything is crashing down on top of us. At every turn, there's a new problem that must be dealt with. There's no break, and when you finally get a reprieve, it never lasts long enough. It happens to all of us. However, we all handle it differently, and it's how we handle it that's most important.

There are people who wear their emotions on their sleeves. Their pain and struggles are painted on their faces and oozes from their pores. They are on the lawn, in front of their flaming house, visibly losing their minds.

Then there are some people who, despite the stress and turmoil going on in their lives, remain pleasant and keep a poker face. Make no mistake, the loss of their home, dog, and fortune pains them, but they know that all of their blessings are given *from* God and can be *taken* by God. When it comes to chasing our dreams, we should aim to be like the second group.

When we chase our dreams and passions, we have decided to take the road less traveled. At some point, we get to a fork in the road where one path leads to what the world wants us to do, and the other leads to God's purpose for us.

At first glance, we see that the path the world has for us is perfectly manicured, and the one that leads to our God-given purpose is noticeably rougher. The grass is unkempt, and a thicket of prickly plants obstruct the path and make it impossible to see farther down the road. At the onset of this rarely used road is a sign.

It reads:

> "WARNING! This path is littered with broken friendships, hollow promises, humbling defeats, and painful sacrifices."

For these reasons, this road lays dormant. In the face of all this, it's easy for most of us to decide to stick with the well-kept path. However, for those of us who walk past that sign and through the prickly plants that are just as sharp as they looked, we find another sign a little ways down the road.

It reads:

"WELCOME! Although the journey ahead is long and treacherous, you will NOT be alone. I WILL be with you. At the end of this road, with your faith in hand, you will step triumphantly into the future I have prepared for you.

— With Love, Your Heavenly Father."

It's this sign that few people see. I'm sure if they had, many more would take this path. But you have to have the fortitude to get past the initial pain the road requires. The dreamers who venture down the unkempt road write the words of the second sign on their hearts. It allows us to remain calm in the midst of the fire. Despite the agony and chaos that may surround us, we can smile because we know it will pass. It's all just part of the journey.

So when things inevitably get rough and everything around you is engulfed in flames, keep calm and have faith. You are not alone.

Remember:

1. Keep calm, even though the journey is long and riddled with potholes and sharp thorns, because you are not alone.

2. Have faith that your current pain will subside, and keep pushing forward.

3. "In my deepest, darkest moments, what really got me through was a prayer. Sometimes my prayer was 'Help me.' Sometimes a prayer was 'Thank you.' What I've discovered is that intimate connection and communication with my creator will always get me through because I know my support, my help, is just a prayer away."

— Iyanla Vanzant

Do You

January 28th, 2016

My curiosity has an unrelenting appetite, and because of this I find myself spending a lot of my free time poring over various articles covering a range of topics. Earlier this week, I was reading an article about Carolina Panther's quarterback, Cam Newton, and it's been weighing heavy on my mind ever since.

It centered on how Newton has evolved into one of if not *the* premier quarterback in the NFL. This bigger profile has brought a higher level of scrutiny. Every action he makes or opinion he expresses is immediately analyzed and critiqued. However, in spite of all this, he's always composed, jovial, and most importantly himself.

One of the most important things we have to realize about this journey is the importance of staying true to who we are. Staying true to who we are doesn't mean we won't change over time, it deals with identifying the changes that are best for us.

We are purpose-driven creatures. We all possess an innate drive, some more than others, to push toward our purpose. It's our duty over the course of our lives to discover what that is. Once we unearth it, we must decide if we want to embrace it.

Imagine that for our entire lives we've been wearing the same blue jacket. It's the same one that just about everyone else wears. We don't know where we got it from, and we just seemed to have always had it. We've never questioned why we wear it because everyone else has the same one. Every once in a while, we see someone with a strange tattered jacket, but usually they're teased or taunted until they get a blue one. However, sometimes they just refuse to conform.

One day, in the distant future, we see them walking down the street draped in an awe-inspiring work of art. Its beauty is beyond comprehension, and we conclude their jacket must've been the brainchild of a fashion savant. We incessantly demand to know where they got such a jacket.

They respond, "Don't you recognize it? It's the same one I've always had."

You see, our dreams are the strange tattered jacket. We all find it at different times, but many of us decide not to wear it, and understandably so. It not only has a pungent odor, but cotton is falling from one of its sides, and one of the sleeves is hanging on by a stitch. After inspecting the jacket further, we realize that even though we have an unusual affection for it, people would mock and look at us strangely if we were to ever wear it. Furthermore, most of us reason that it would take more time, energy, and resources to make it wearable than we are willing to invest. So we put it aside and put back on the blue jacket that everybody else is wearing.

We decide to fit into someone else's dream instead of wearing our own.

When we choose to chase our dreams, we have decided to mend that tattered jacket. With each thread sewn and patch added, we discover something new about ourselves. At last, when we finally put that finished jacket on, we're ready for all the attention that it will bring because we have endured so much while creating it.

Its uniqueness will cause others to ask, "Why are they so confident?" or "Why are they having so much fun?" But the real question they want answered but will never ask is, "Why don't I have a jacket like that?"

The thing is, they can—but first they have to put in the time and work to create it. When they do so, they will mature; learn more about themselves, and how to help lead others to do the same.

A couple of years ago, Cam Newton was Carolina's starting and franchise quarterback but was not voted team captain. Unusual, but he lacked the maturity to lead at the time. His jacket still needed some work. Now, a few years later, he's leading his team to the Super Bowl.

After we have tailored our jacket and customized it to accommodate all our needs for the time being, because the tailoring of our jacket is a lifelong process, it won't matter what people have to say about it—because we're comfortable in it. We are comfortable in our own skin and with the decisions that brought us to this point. When our day in the sun comes, we will shine even brighter due to that.

Remember:

1. Toss aside the "blue jacket" everyone wants you to wear, and create your own.

2. The more comfortable we are in our skin, the brighter we shine when we arrive at our dreams.

3. "Always be yourself, express yourself, have faith in yourself, do not go out and look for a successful personality and duplicate it."
   — Bruce Lee

Rerouting...

February 12th, 2016

I started last week with so much heaped atop my plate I didn't know where to begin. A myriad of unfocused thoughts intertwining with numerous goals I wanted completed by the end of the month made my mind quite a mess. But let's start from the beginning.

For all intents and purposes, my January was lackluster. I came down with a severe case of procrastination. I sensed the symptoms coming along, but I did nothing to fight back and decided to ride it out. It began with an unusual willingness to push aside projects I was working on in favor of extracurricular activities, such as going out, watching movies, and playing NBA 2K16. That was pretty much my January 2016.

As I expected, once January passed, my passion finally started fighting back against the procrastination infection. I woke up on the 1st of February with a soul-shaking urge to be productive. However, it's not that easy to flip the switch. First, a cleanse was in order. So I began a week-long fast. I gave up sugar, including juice, red meat, and most importantly, NBA 2K16, which had eaten up a lot of my January nights.

Rerouting...

I had to get back to neutral. I was too far gone. My devotional that Monday morning started everything. It was appropriately titled "Fast and Pray." I like to think it was a friendly nudge from God, who was saying, "You had your fun, now let's get back to work."

At the onset of my week-long fast, I prayed that God would help "redirect me" so that I could clearly see how to accomplish everything I wanted by my February 28th deadline.

Naturally, the first couple of days were the hardest. I found myself staring at the Xbox One controller, itching to get a 2K16 game in, or thirsting for something besides water to wash down my chicken dinner. However, by Wednesday, I started to feel more like my old self. Instead of playing video games, I used that time to critically read Stephen King's book *On Writing: A Memoir of the Craft.*

I had started reading it late last summer, but it wasn't my copy, and the owner eventually wanted it back. Recently, however, an author, who had taken an interest in my work suggested I read it. She said I *needed* to read it if I seriously wanted to sharpen my craft. So, of course, I ordered my copy.

Armed with a blue ballpoint pen, I dove in and was immediately thankful. If my heart could explode due to happiness, my room would have resembled a rough night in the ER.

I'm always striving to get better, but figuring out how to do so is not always simple. Looking back, this conundrum played a large role in my succumbing to the procrastination bug in January. The author who recommended King's book to me gave me another book on writing on Thursday, and I ordered *another one* (DJ Khaled voice) based on a recommendation in King's book.

Just like that, by Saturday I was replenishing my well with the knowledge of the greats who came before me. By Sunday, the end of my fast, I knew exactly what I had to do to be in the position I wanted to be in by the end of the month.

We can never stray too far off track when God is our GPS. If we truly have a desire to get back on course, we will. However, we first have to be *willing* to part with the things that facilitated our detour, and then immerse ourselves again in our craft. Let's not forget this is a long journey. We all have Januaries like mine, it just comes down to how we respond.

In all of my posts where I discuss my journey, I do so in hopes that someone can pull something out that will help them keep going. I don't have all the answers, nor would I ever claim to. I'm only relaying my thoughts and experiences as I find my way.

P.S. – I will be releasing an e-book in the near future featuring the first 11 *Turner Street* stories, re-edited and all in one place. More details will be available in the coming weeks!

Remember:

1. Sometimes we have to take a detour in order to get back on course.

2. When we allow God to be our GPS, we won't stay lost for long.

3. "See any detour as an opportunity to experience new things."

— H. Jackson Brown, Jr.

Who's Listening?

February 25th, 2016

Everyone has a story. But how often do we really listen to someone else's? We can get so caught up in ourselves that we forget everyone around us has their own beliefs, aspirations, and sorrows. It wasn't until a couple of years ago that I really started actively listening instead of simply hearing. I quickly learned that a genuine interest in the stories of others helps to sharpen my own ideas and dreams.

As I began to listen, more and more people fed me stories. I became a collector of sorts. And like any collector, I needed to understand what I had in my possession. So I asked questions such as, "Why did you do this, instead of that?" or "Was it really all worth it?"

With each probe, I learned something new, and more times than not, it's fascinating. The person leaving their story with me does so with a smile. Because who doesn't like to be listened to?

We all require an audience at some point. We need someone to hear what we've done and gone through. We need someone to know we existed. Not everyone's story will be written about and discussed in classrooms. But that doesn't make any of our lives any less meaningful. The single mother of three is just as important as the revolutionary. One is trying to change the world while the other raises those who will inherit it. We should honor everyone's story by being willing to listen when they're ready to share it.

I recently had a conversation with a remarkable young woman whose story really struck me. She talked of her trials and tribulations and her fight to overcome them. As riveting as her tale was, it was how she ended it that was truly unforgettable.

She smiled and said, "I keep falling and falling, but I always get up, because it's not about me but what God needs me to do."

I loved this for a multitude of reasons, but most importantly because it illustrates that our lives are not ours alone. What we do directly and indirectly affects the people around us. Achieving our dreams isn't just about us, but about those who will see us and interact with us along the way.

Stories have power, and our stories can inspire those who come behind us. It could be our children, relatives, or some stranger we're talking to while standing in line. We're all trying to find our way, and many who are ahead of us or traveling alongside us have stories that can benefit us, stories that will motivate us.

The keys to our success are in listening and comprehending what we heard. Think about a time when someone shared a story with you and you were really listening—not to respond, but to learn. Now think about how you felt after that interaction. It's usually immensely satisfying. It's a win-win. Not only have they passed their story on to us, but we are wiser because of it. If we are willing to listen, we have no idea what we might learn and what missteps we may avoid.

A favorite saying of my mother's is "if you don't hear, you'll feel." I've always loved its simplicity. We set ourselves up for unavoidable pain when we refuse to take heed. Of course, even if we listen we may decide to ignore the advice and take our chances. But as long as we listen, we give ourselves the chance to make an informed decision.

I learned a while ago that the road to ruin is paved with the skeletons of those who were unable to listen. An escapable fate if we just open our ears and pay attention.

Remember:

1. Take the time to listen to the stories of those who are willing to share.

2. It's a privilege to hear someone's story and should be treated as such.

3. "I like to listen. I have learned a great deal from listening carefully. Most people never listen."
   — Ernest Hemingway

(P.S. Keep an eye out for information on the soon-to-be-released e-book comprised of the first 11 *Turner Street* short stories...)

No Worries

March 10th, 2016

Bob Marley famously sang in "Three Little Birds" about how there's no need to worry, because in due time every little thing will turn out just fine. We should take that message to heart. We worry about a lot of things, to the point of exhaustion. The worst part is that most of the time, the thing we're worrying about is completely out of our control, but that doesn't stop us. It's an addiction, and like all addictions, we have to first admit we have a problem before we can treat it.

In middle school, I ran for class president. To say that I *ran* is actually giving me more credit than I deserve. I was really pushed into candidacy. At lunch, a couple of periods before the candidates were to give their speeches to the entire middle school, the principal approached me and said he had nominated me. I was giving a speech in a couple of hours.

I can't remember how I initially responded, but I remember how I felt. I remember a deep, sinking feeling in the pit of my stomach and my mind nearly combusting as it raced to find a believable excuse. It was no use. The principal said the decision was final. He explained that he had watched me interact with my peers and thought I'd be a good choice.

Naturally, I was worried. However, an interesting thing happened over the next couple of hours as I put together a speech. I started to get excited. I took a closer look at the reasons behind why I was worried in the first place and realized that none of them were things I could actually control. At the end of the day, whether I won or lost would come down to how my peers perceived me, and how others think of you is *completely* out of your control. All I could do was state my case and hope for the best.

This realization put me at ease, and the words flowed from my fingertips and onto the page. When the time came, I delivered my speech with passion and conviction, two things I never lack. I don't remember that speech particularly well—it was a while ago—but I did win the vice presidency. It was a great gig, especially for someone who didn't plan to run in the first place. I got the perks of being class president without the responsibility.

I always remind myself of this story when I'm worrying too much. My worrying did not help my situation, and once I realized that, I was able to find success.

Imagine our worries as a massive, snarling beast. However, we've never seen this beast. It's locked behind a door. We think we can hear its murderous cries and violent scratches against the door. We imagine it with all of its fangs and sharp claws, waiting for us to foolishly open the door so it can shred us to pieces.

Despite these fears, we have to open that door.

When we do, we see that the beast was nothing but a puppy gnawing at the doorframe. In actuality, our worries are far smaller and less fearsome than we imagine. But if we don't open up that door, and many of us don't, we will never see the truth. We will forever be bogged down by senseless worries and imaginings.

A couple of days ago, I was approached by a respected man in his field, and he said he felt compelled to tell me, "Stop worrying, God has a plan."

His words immediately eased my mind and reminded me of my middle-school campaign. I had again allowed myself to worry about things that were out of my control, and it was time to let them go. His words actually served as the catalyst for this post.

There will always be things to worry about, and it's up to us to decide whether we will waste our time and energy on them or not. We cannot allow our dreams to be deferred by imaginary beasts and senseless worries.

(P.S. It's almost time for ***Turner Street: Where the Monsters in the Closet are Real***, a collection of short stories, to be released as an e-book. Check back next week for more details!)

Remember:

1. Worrying gets nothing done.

2. Our worries are usually much smaller in reality than they are in our minds.

3. "Therefore I tell you, do not worry about your life, what you will eat or drink; or about your body, what you will wear. Is not your life more than food and the body more than clothes? Look at the birds of the air; they do not sow or reap or store away in barns, and yet your heavenly father feeds them. Are you not much more valuable than they?"

— Matthew 6:25-26

Ramblings on Love – August 14th, 2019 – 3:06AM

I love the idea of love. That is something I've known about myself for a long time now. It's really the idea of being the recipient of unconditional love from another that's so intoxicating. Why? I suppose because that's the love that God wishes to have with us and has planted a yearning for such a love in our hearts.

I don't think such a love is possible between humans, at least not in the long run. I think for humans, unconditional love becomes conditional and then evaporates into the ether as time passes. I've thought about this at great length (exactly how much time is unknown) and I've decided (for the time being, because God has a way of changing the thoughts of man in an instant) an unconditional love between two humans is *only* possible if both surrender their pride and ego to God.

It's only then, as equals, that they can stand together in harmony against the forces of life that wish to tear them apart. However, that unity, as special and as powerful as it may be, is only temporal, not eternal. We come into this world alone and not un-

Ramblings on Love – August 14th, 2019 – 3:06AM

der our own volition (well, to an extent, because since we are all God's spirit we have to believe that our grander self at some point asked to be born).

When we leave this world it will be alone, but along the way, we have the choice to love recklessly and passionately, and we must. If we are not loving, we are not living. But love in this fallen world will bring pain. Pain so great that every breath becomes a chore and makes the mere thought of existence unbearable. Such pain is only bearable because the other side of the spectrum is so sublime. I can only imagine what love is like sans pain and the corruption of sin. It is indeed something to look forward to.

How long does it take one to fall in love? Can it really be in an instant? I must admit that I, unsurprisingly but proudly, fall into the camp of Love at First Sight. When the soul knows, the soul knows. This note has been all over the place. I'm tired, I'm going to sleep lol.

Nevertheless, I will finish my point. I don't think our human idea of love is necessary to live a fulfilled life, but I think God's

Ramblings on Love – August 14th, 2019 – 3:06AM

love expressed through humans can lead to unimaginably fulfilling relationships. Those relationships make life worth living.

    Have faith, my friend, I love you.

— R.S. Veira

Keep Calm & Enjoy the Journey 3

March 31st, 2016

A few weekends ago, I published my first e-book, *Turner Street: Where the Monsters in the Closet are Real*, and after its release, I was faced with a hodgepodge of emotions. I was insanely excited, but at the same time, I was incredibly nervous. It was similar to when I launched this blog—despite the amount of work I had put into it, I had no idea how it would be received.

It was during this time of uncertainty that I was reminded of that wise man's words from a few weeks ago: "Stop worrying, God has a plan." As I remembered these words, my anxiety melted away and I was left with unparalleled joy. I had set a goal, to publish an e-book, and had reached it. There is no better feeling.

Last summer, I started playing around with the idea of compiling the *Turner Street* short stories. It was just an idea for a long time, mainly because my sole focus was on finding an agent for my first manuscript. However, by the end of the year, I knew I had to publish something that I could present to people as an example of my writing.

So after my lackadaisical January, I began to put everything together. I took the core stories I wanted to include and again immersed myself in that world. I expanded some of them and removed unnecessary fluff. When I finally finished, I reached out to a woman by the name of Laurie Wright on Fiverr, and she put together the book's amazing cover.

Like everything, it was a process.

Our dreams start off as faint ideas. They sound great, and we're greatly enthused by their freshness. However, this enthusiasm is dampened when we realize the amount of time and effort it requires to bring them into reality.

But the truth is, no matter the cost, it's worth it.

There's no other way to explain it. The feeling I had when I saw my e-book finished and my name at the bottom of the cover is unexplainable. I have never been more proud nor thankful in my life.

During its free promotion, *Turner Street* was #1 on both Amazon's Top 100 Free Fantasy Anthologies & Short Stories and Young Adult Short Reads. The free promotion ended last Friday (3/25/16) at midnight, and it is now back at regular price. I encourage you all to check it out.

I'm truly thankful for this blog and for the people who take the time out of their day to read my thoughts and stories. Without that, *Turner Street* would never have happened.

At each break in my journey, after I have accomplished a goal, I like to reflect on the process that got me there. The one thing I took away from publishing this e-book was that everything seems so far away until we get there.

When I seriously started to put *Turner Street* together, I had to learn what an e-book of that genre looked like, sold for, and how to market it. All of that at once was overwhelming, and the end goal looked to be on the distant horizon. I knew the key to reaching that goal was to keep my head in the work and hold myself accountable. I did a little research every day. I talked to other authors who had published e-books and learned their methodology and applied it to my own.

By not focusing solely on the end goal but instead on the daily task at hand, I was able to finish. I kept myself accountable by writing a "P.S." after each of my blog posts for a month, teasing about an e-book in the near future. I couldn't let you down, the people who support me, and that drove me onward. Eventually, I looked up and *Turner Street* was done.

That's the key to finishing anything. We must keep our noses to the grindstone and hold ourselves accountable. Before we know it, we will arrive at our destination.

Remember:

1. It's a process. Nothing significant is accomplished immediately.

2. Embrace wholeheartedly the goal at hand, and it will eventually be accomplished.

3. "Have patience. All things are difficult before they become easy."

— Saadi

Turner Street: Where the Monsters in the Closet are Real is available on Amazon Kindle and Kindle App!

Mamba Out

April 14th, 2016

Kobe Bryant scored 60 points last night in the final game of his 20th season. When you really sit down and analyze the performance and all that went into it, it's almost too incredible and/or fantastical to be a believable end to a movie, let alone a storied career. But it happened, and it was one of the most miraculous things I have ever witnessed.

At the start of this NBA season, I wrote a post focused on Kobe's final seasons—at the time, it wasn't official that he was retiring. However, after the announcement, I dreaded April 13th. It would be the day that I would say goodbye to a childhood hero, my basketball idol. Little did I know that on that night, he would remind me and millions of others why we believed in him in the first place.

Kobe's competitiveness, work ethic, and drive made him an easy role model as a kid. At some level, I knew if I ever wanted to achieve my dreams, I would have to possess those things. However, not everyone saw it that way. I was often asked how I could idolize him. "He's a ball hog," they would say. "He's selfish. All he cares about is himself." I get it, he's not perfect.

The thing is, when it comes to any of our role models, they all fall short of perfection. We don't idolize them because they're perfect, but because they possess qualities that we see in ourselves and hope to sharpen, or they possess ones that we hold in high regard and hope to obtain.

Last night, I watched a legend in his last game, a spectacle in itself with a 20-minute pregame ceremony in his honor, fight back against father time one last time. The world wanted an unforgettable performance, and he delivered. Despite two consecutive season-ending injuries, he delivered.

After a 16-65 season, all I wanted to see was Kobe go out fighting. The Utah Jazz were one game away from making the playoffs, and the chances of this game getting out of hand were high. Things didn't look any better with Kobe starting 0-5 from the field, missing his first five shots. I was reminded this was not the Kobe I grew up watching, but I was mistaken.

His body may have worn down, but his competitiveness, work ethic, and drive shone brighter than ever. At 37 years old, he left everything on the floor and carried the Lakers to one final win, making big shot after big shot. He reminded us that the remarkable is always possible if we invest the time and work into our craft. Can you ask any more from a role model?

Life is funny in how it plays out, the way it offers us chances at redemption. Kobe's final game was against a team that nearly 20 years ago forced him into one of the most embarrassing games of his career. As a rookie, in the playoffs, he air-balled four times in the closing moments against the Utah Jazz, and the Lakers lost the series because of it. Twenty years later, he scores 60 points in his farewell game against the same organization and everything comes full circle.

If there is anything we can take away from Kobe's career it's that no matter how great the adversity or how long the odds, we can still come out on top if our determination never falters. The most divisive player in league history left his last game to a chorus of loving chants, and with the respect of all.

For those of us who have the courage to chase our dreams, there's nothing better than to see someone fully realize theirs.

Mamba Out

Enjoying the View
April 28th, 2016

One of my favorite things to do is watch the rise of dream chasers. I love tracking their ascent and witnessing them achieve what they set out to do. "Learning from the Greats I & II" are two of my favorite blog posts for that reason. It's no surprise, then, that this week has been especially good to me. Drake's fourth solo studio album, *VIEWS*, will be released Friday, and it could very well be the crowning achievement of his career thus far.

This is intriguing on many levels. The first being that we are currently witnessing someone perform at the top of their game. It's similar to watching Kobe in the mid-2000s, or Michael Jordan in the 90s. Better yet, it's like watching Steph Curry now. It's inspiring and transfixing. It should make us want to perfect our own crafts just to see what we're capable of when we are at our peak.

However, it's easy to see those at the top of their game and get sidetracked by the fame and money their talents generate. The thing is, it shouldn't be about either but about doing what we were born to do at the highest level we are capable of achieving.

For example, I sat down to write this post, and just sitting be-

Enjoying the View

hind the computer filled me with a sense of fulfillment. There was nothing else I would rather be doing than writing; be it short stories, novels, scripts, or blog posts. Writing is what I love to do, and honing that skill is an obsession. Money has a way of finding you by itself when you are exceptional at what you do. You don't have to chase it.

As we all know, we don't achieve anything significant overnight. I had a fascinating conversation with an engineer earlier this week that highlighted that fact. When I first met him, he nonchalantly claimed to be one of the best in his field.

Naturally, I was intrigued. I peppered him with questions. He explained to me how he wakes up every morning and begins writing code at 6:30 AM. He codes in the morning, afternoon, and evening. He stressed the necessity of hard work by illustrating how few of his peers would never even consider waking up early enough to start coding by 6:30 AM. That's what separates him, he claimed: the willingness to do whatever it takes to be great at what he does.

He was also a Dallas Mavericks fan, and he used his fandom to further drive home his point. The point he made that resonated with me the most centered on the work ethic of Mavericks star Dirk Nowitzki. He claimed he'd pay to watch Dirk practice and asked me, "How many people do you think would pay to sit and watch Dirk practice?" I said, "Not many."

He agreed that there would be some, but the majority would rather watch Dirk in an actual game and would rather ignore the preparation needed to produce at such a high level. That's the separator. Only those who truly want to be great at what they do obsess over the process of being great. They see the beauty in the process, and it's a beauty that transcends and links all disciplines. It's a beauty that allows a top engineer to appreciate, and on a certain level understand, the preparation of a top athlete.

We cannot only find enjoyment at the end of our journey, but we must also find it in the process it takes to get there. If we are unable to find enjoyment in the process, then we'll never reach the end.

The journey to our dreams has too many snares and pitfalls for us to overcome if we are doing it solely to be rich or famous. Of course, one can achieve fame and fortune without doing what they love, but why invest the time and energy in achieving those things if we are miserable in their pursuit?

As great as those two things are, they are fleeting. If we allow them to be our motivation, we will end up unfulfilled. That's a hard truth to hear because the pursuit of money and fame drives so many of us, and that's a true tragedy.

So as the world prepares for Drake's most anticipated album to date, let us see it for what it is: the culmination of years of work and sacrifices. Let it inspire us to hone our own crafts so that one day we may produce great work of our own.

Remember:

1. There's more to success than fame and fortune.

2. If we don't enjoy the process, we'll never reach our destination.

3. "Excellence is a continuous process and not an accident."

— A. P. J. Abdul Kalam

Keep Calm & Enjoy the Journey 4
July 7th, 2016

I was once told an interesting story that taught me how to handle the good and bad days we encounter.

It begins with a boy sitting at the dinner table waiting for dinner to be served. His mother places a large plate of steamed broccoli in front of him, his least favorite vegetable. The boy struggles to finish his meal. Over the course of the following couple of days, the boy's mother prepares a balanced meal made up of vegetables, meat, and a sweet dessert. The boy pleasantly eats it. At the end of the week, the boy's mother gives him a slice of apple pie à la mode for dinner with a smile. The boy asks no questions and dives in.

The moral of the story is simple. Some days, we have to put up with a lot and force down the vegetables. Other days, everything is going our way and we happily devour our pie à la mode. But most of the time, we have a balance of the two.

I'm not sure when I first heard that story, but nonetheless, it stuck with me. It's funny, the stories we remember from when we were younger, and how they manage to stay with us throughout the years.

Turner Street: The Cain Seed, the second book in the *Turner Street Chronicles*, comes out next week, and its release has prompted me to evaluate the process of writing it in order to prepare for future projects.

It took me longer than I would have hoped to finish the last couple of stories in *Cain Seed*. It was during those days that I felt as if I had been served a sloppy plate of coleslaw, my least favorite food. The ideas came slowly. I couldn't see how the story was going to end. However, I forced myself to write. I sat down and managed a sentence or two before I had to close my laptop for a while. This went on for days at a time.

I ate coleslaw for about a month before I finally managed to get a balanced meal, and *Cain Seed*'s end started to come into focus. At last, I finished the antepenultimate story, currently titled *The Infirmary: Monica's Testament*. Once completed, the final two stories pretty much wrote themselves. During those days writing was easy again, and it was like I was feasting on apple pie à la mode, my favorite dessert.

Writer's block is not a new phenomenon, but dealing with it can be tricky. I've addressed it a few times throughout my blog. Each case is different and has its own solution. In this particular case, I figured that if I was able to get at least something down on the page, it was better than nothing. I told myself, "I may not like it, but it's good for me."

When we have a string of bad days where we are served only vegetables, we tend to push our plates away and wish that we were eating dessert instead. However, what we should be doing is trudging through our meal and appreciating it for what it is, a meal. It's a chance to grow and learn more about ourselves. In all honesty, the bad days may very well be the most important. Without them, we are unable to sharpen our will, test our determination, and prove our love for our crafts.

Handling bad days properly prepares us for future worse ones and helps us really appreciate the good ones. As any parent will agree, we rob ourselves of the chance of being our best selves if we don't finish our vegetables. If we truly desire to see our dreams come to fruition, we have to see our bad days in a different light; we have to see them not only as an opportunity to get better at what we love to do but as a chance to prove how much we love doing what we do.

Even though what we love to do may be difficult sometimes, we must do it all the same, because we love it. Love always perseveres. With this in mind, those veggies should go down much easier from now on.

(**P.S.** Book two in the *Turner Street Chronicles*, *Turner Street: The Cain Seed*, will be released next Friday!)

Remember:

1. The bad days may very well be the most important.

2. Use the bad days to showcase your love for your craft.

3. "Most of the important things in the world have been accomplished by people who have kept on trying when there seemed to be no hope at all."
— Dale Carnegie

In Due Time

August 25th, 2016

There is never a moment in our lives when God is not working, however, we can lose sight of that at times. It's easy to think that during the monotony that can sometimes consume our lives, God has forgotten about us—if only for a moment. And in this state of bewilderment, we have to truly trust in His plan.

Last week, I had the opportunity to begin shooting a short film I wrote. For that to come to fruition, it took the better part of the summer. Actors' schedules had to line up, we had to find a place to shoot, and of course, we still had to do rehearsals. It was a process, and during this ordeal, there were periods of time where nothing was accomplished. Weeks went by where we could not hold rehearsals because of conflicting engagements. There came a point where it seemed like the project would never happen, at least not with the current cast.

One day earlier in the month, in the midst of all this, I had a talk with the producer/editor of the film, and we discussed whether or not we were going to push forward with the project. Enthusiasm in the cast was waning with each passing week. It was a passion project, after all, meaning no one was getting paid, so once the passion dried up, everything was in jeopardy.

Thankfully, the producer let me know that earlier that same day, he had talked to a musician who lives in a cabin in a forested area. The musician just so happened to be looking to use the cabin as a place where creatives could create. This included using it for film projects. So we decided that he, the producer, would check out the location. He sent me a video of the place, and it was perfect. As we began to lay out our plans for the shoot later that week, I couldn't help but think about how just hours ago I not only had no idea where we were going to shoot, but I wasn't even sure if we were going to shoot at all.

God's timing is perfect. That's hard to accept at times because we crave instant gratification from our actions. We want things so badly sometimes that we don't realize our eagerness could lead to the failure of our plans. Some things must come in time, because only in time can everything fit together how it needs to.

For example, if we had begun shooting at my apartment in a rush to get the film done, we would have missed the opportunity to shoot in a location that fits the script. Our project would have missed its chance to be as good as it could be.

When we rush into things that we think we deserve without doing our due diligence and seeking God's guidance, we rob the experience of being as great as it could have been.

Now, by no means am I advocating laying around and waiting for opportunity to seize us. We must continue to grind, to hone our skills, and to reach out for potential opportunities. But, at the same time, we must not rush into or force them. By doing this, we show God that we are doing the best we can with what we have and that we trust him to open the door for us when the time is right.

It's then that things begin to fall into place, emails get answered, and the right jobs are offered. Patience is just as important as work ethic.

I was on set last Thursday to shoot a short film I wrote and had the amazing opportunity to direct—it was a blessing in every sense. Not only was my vision coming to life before my eyes, but I was in a position to take advantage of the opportunity.

During the time it took to find the right location and coordinate schedules, I was able to complete script rewrites and figure out how I wanted the short film to look. I did my best to be productive during the time we had nothing going on so that when it was time to move, I would be ready.

That's the key. We have to continue to prepare while God works behind the scenes. He will make a way when it's time.

Remember:

1. Patience is just as important as work ethic.

2. Don't rush into things you think you deserve, but allow God to bless you with what you really deserve.

3. "Patience is not simply the ability to wait—it's how we behave while we're waiting."

— Joyce Meyer

Ramblings on Life – January 18th, 2020 – 6:55PM

Closure is an interesting concept. We long for it in many situations, but I don't even think we know what it really is. I think closure ultimately is the willingness to let go of something in faith. You have faith that what is yours is yours; that what God brings together, no man can separate. So when things don't go as we hoped they would, we can rest assured that they went just as they needed to. I like that idea, and it seems right.

Have faith, my friend, I love you.

— R.S. Veira

A Satisfying Ending
November 24th, 2016

It's been a little while since my last post, and a lot has transpired in that time. I finished the final collection of *Turner Street* stories, the short film I wrote and directed wrapped, and I attended my first writer's convention. I wanted to update all of you on my progress and share some things I learned from each experience.

I attended the World Fantasy Convention (WFC) in October. It was hosted in Columbus, Ohio. Until about early June, I had no plans of attending, and in all honesty, I didn't even know it existed. It wasn't until I finished Brandon Sanderson's *The Reckoners* trilogy that my eyes were opened. After completing the trilogy, I was curious about the author. The trilogy was well-written, fast-paced, and genuinely intriguing.

While perusing Mr. Sanderson's *About Me* page on his website, I learned that he met his agent and many industry friends by attending conferences such as the World Fantasy Convention. Combine that with my obsession to better my craft and it's no surprise I ended up in Columbus. I registered and bought my ticket a few days later.

A Satisfying Ending

The convention was an amazing experience. I went in with a simple goal in mind: network. When I used to play basketball, I surrounded myself with basketball players—people who were as serious about the game as myself. I trained with people with similar goals, people who would push me to be better, and I'd do the same for them. It only made sense that if I was serious about writing, a similar process was necessary.

My first day at the convention was spent browsing the dealer rooms and attending a couple of panels I found interesting. However, things didn't really take off until later in the evening when I spent some time at the bar.

Before I attended WFC, I did a bit of research on what to expect from my first writer's convention. The common thread amongst them all was to spend as much time at the bar as possible. This was where writers, agents, and publishers would congregate like animals at the watering hole. It was here that I met the people I would spend most of my time with. It was a humbling experience to spend time with writers who had work published and the agents who represented them.

It was also an incredible learning experience. I was able to pick their brains and gather nuggets of useful information. I even had the opportunity to pitch my novel and was asked to send the full manuscript. My time at WFC was invigorating and well spent.

I highly recommend attending conventions like this, or workshops, to those who are serious about whatever they do. Not only do you get the opportunity to mingle with like-minded people, but you get an up-close and personal idea of how your industry works.

In the time between my last post and now, I managed to finish *Turner Street: Anomalies* (coming this December). What I've come to really appreciate about *Turner Street* is how it showcases the progression of my writing. Each collection is a great representation of my writing at that point in time. Each book forced me to tackle new challenges. For example, this final entry in the *Turner Street Chronicles* gave me the opportunity to work on endings. A satisfying ending can make or break a story, in my opinion, and I think *Anomalies* brings everything home.

Finally, my short film titled *For Better or Worse* wrapped earlier this month and was one of my better experiences of the year. I witnessed firsthand the collaboration needed in order to make a film come to life. Developing the patience and leadership required to take my written vision and put it on film was my biggest takeaway. *For Better or Worse* is currently in post-production and should be done by the end of the year.

It's about that time of year when we reflect and give thanks. I'm thankful for this journey and all of you who are on it with me.

Happy Thanksgiving!

Remember:

1. Research conferences and workshops that you can attend to help better yourself and your craft.

2. No matter the experience, find something positive to take away from it.

3. "Be thankful for what you have; you'll end up having more. If you concentrate on what you don't have, you will never, ever have enough."

— Oprah Winfrey

P.S. – *Turner Street: Anomalies* will be out next month! In the meantime, catch up on the first two books in the *Turner Street Chronicles*!

Balancing Expectations

January 12th, 2017

I was talking to an actor friend a few days ago, and we stumbled upon the subject of time. He's got some years on me and is a vet of the entertainment industry, so naturally, I pick his brain when given the opportunity. As I peppered him with questions, he gamely responded with well-thought-out answers, and in the midst of one of these responses, he said he had taken 12 years off from acting. Twelve years.

This immediately sent the gears in my head spinning. It reminded me of just how long life is. Life is not short. Our time here only seems short to us in hindsight. Think about it, a single year is a considerable amount of time. To be precise, it's 8,760 hours, or 365 days (excluding leap years). Twelve years is 105,120 hours, or 4,380 days. What happens if in 12 years we're not where we want to be?

It's no secret that time is an obsession of mine. There's a voice in the back of my head constantly prodding, "Am I using my time wisely?" It's a blessing and a curse.

For example, two years ago I wrote out a four-year plan, and

Balancing Expectations

every December I jot down my three main objectives for the coming year. I always have a pretty clear idea of what I should be focusing on; I consider that a blessing. However, my obsession with time can also lead to excruciating stress. If I fail to complete one of the tasks in the designated time I've given myself, I can quickly find myself in a rut. Which, of course, takes time to get out, thus wasting even more time. It can be a vicious cycle.

I recently found myself in such a cycle after I failed to finish a script in the time I allotted myself. I was struggling to get back on track when I had the aforementioned conversation with my friend. Our talk reminded me that this journey is a marathon, not a sprint.

We can sometimes get ahead of ourselves in the pursuit of our dreams. We feel that we have to achieve our dreams now, and that any longer than a couple of years means failure. This is where we get into trouble. We set unreasonable expectations for ourselves, and when we don't meet them, we're devastated. The key is to manage these expectations appropriately.

Dream big, but in doing so, understand that the bigger the dream, the more time and effort it will require to bring it to fruition. As dreamers, we have to believe that any day could be *the* day that changes everything, but we must also understand that any day could be just that, a regular day, and our time may not come for months, years, or even decades. I believe our ability to balance these expectations will ultimately determine if we achieve our dreams.

When I sat down to write this post, I took some time to look back on my past posts. The purpose of this was twofold: I was in need of inspiration, and I was curious to see how things had changed for me since the early days of this blog.

It didn't take long to find what I was looking for.

I laughed as I read my earlier posts, reminded of how I wrote them in my parents' basement just two years ago—imagining doing what I'm doing now.

As I skimmed these posts, I was reminded of my mindset at the time. My goal every day was to do something, no matter how small, to improve as a writer and prepare for my move to Los Angeles. I did that for a year; it was a long year. Looking back, it's clear that that preparation made everything I'm doing now possible.

Who knows where we will be in a year's time, let alone 12. But what I can tell you is that if we continue to believe that any day could be *the* day, and at the same time temper our obscene optimism with an understanding that it could be a while before we breakthrough, we will obtain the serene balance necessary to achieve our dreams. Who knows how long it will take for us to arrive, but regardless, we should enjoy every step.

Remember:

1. The journey is a marathon, not a sprint.

2. Learn to properly manage your expectations.

3. "Don't let the fear of the time it will take to accomplish something stand in the way of your doing it. The time will pass anyway; we might just as well put that passing time to the best possible use."

— Earl Nightingale

Keep Calm & Enjoy the Journey 5
April 20th, 2017

For the entirety of March, motivation was scarce. This famine was not brought on by a lack of work. On the contrary, there was more than enough of that, but it was as if someone had reached into my soul and snatched my will.

Writer's block had officially taken hold by the second week of March. I've written at length about how best to beat stagnation, conquer a rut, or (in my case) vanquish writer's block. None of that worked this time. Instead, it clung to me like a fungus. All attempts to shake it caused it to grow and lash out even more viciously until I was engulfed and left immobilized.

It became painfully awkward to sit at my desk. My laptop screen watched me, begging me to fill the page it offered while I looked on vacantly, only producing a word or two before slamming it shut, drunk off the unholy cocktail of frustration, embarrassment, and self-loathing. I couldn't write.

A curious thing happens to us when the thing we love is suddenly taken away. The world dulls. Nothing pops, and our days become a monotonous march into nothingness. I had lost the ability to create, and *that* was killing me.

I woke up Tuesday, and my first clear thought was, "No more." As I do in times of joy, contentment, or pain, I turned to God. I said, "Lord, I can't shake it this time. I need You."

And God answered.

The ironic thing about me needing motivation is that I have a blog dedicated to it (over 70,000 words!). However, for the past five to six months, I've been working to get so many things rolling that I haven't been actively posting.

I had forgotten what was on my blog.

So on Tuesday, after my conversation with the Big Guy, I suddenly had the urge to update things. Add a few buttons here, link a few things there, and while I was doing that, I started reading what I had written. I started with "Keep Calm & Enjoy the Journey 4," and it struck me like it never had before. I immediately relived the anxiety and uncertainty of that time. I started to dig deeper and uncovered more, losing myself in my own words and taking a trip back in time.

Sometimes you have to step back and remind yourself that you have struggled mightily and have overcome before, and you can overcome again. The fungus started to loosen. I was reminded in "Keep Calm & Enjoy the Journey 2" of my first days in LA and the year of preparation leading up to them. And as I read, I knew what I had to do. I had to write a blog post.

The revelation was so simple that all I could do was laugh, and with that laughter, the fungus lost hold and color was injected back into the world. I wrote this with a grin that stretched from ear to ear; it couldn't have been any more cathartic. The words sputtered at first but soon flowed, like God had turned the faucet back on. I was at peace.

When I first started my blog, I repeated the same mantra to myself, "If only one person reads this and it helps them to keep going, then I've done my job." I've never felt more strongly about that than I do right now. So many dreams die because the dreamer loses motivation and forgets how far they have already come.

You have come so far from where you once were. Keep going.

It's funny, I wrote these blog posts for you—the Dreamer out there—and it didn't even occur to me that I was writing them for myself as well, in case I ever got lost.

Whatever it is that's holding you up, it will pass, believe me.

Remember:

1. Motivation comes and goes. Stay the course regardless.

2. No matter what it is, it will pass.

3. "If you're going through hell, keep going."

— Winston Churchill

P.S. – I have a couple of projects coming soon that I can't wait to share with you! I'll be in touch.

Blessings at Hand

June 30th, 2017

As sad as it is to say, we have an unfortunate tendency of allowing blessings to go unnoticed and underappreciated. We'll even try to find ways to poke holes in our blessings; we reason that nothing can be *that* good. It's a tragic habit.

I finished my first feature-length screenplay a month ago, and until recently, I found myself at an impasse. I had been given a blessing that I was not fully appreciating. After I finish any project, I'm usually immediately thankful, and there are a couple of reasons for this. First, the toiling with and prodding of my imagination had at last given birth to something coherent. Secondly, I'm again reminded that it is possible to create something that had previously not existed.

However, after completing the screenplay, I was so focused on what to do with it, specifically selling it, that I didn't allow myself to fully acknowledge the blessing at hand. It wasn't until earlier this week during my morning devotional that I began to fully comprehend what was happening. I was reading in the Book of James and zeroed in on a few verses.

James 4:13-15:

> *"Now listen, you who say, 'Today or tomorrow we will go to this or that city, spend a year there, carry on business and make money.' Why, you don't even know what will happen tomorrow. What is your life? You are a mist that appears for a short while and then vanishes. Instead you ought to say, 'If this is the Lord's will, we will live and do this or that.'"*

I believe that our gifts and talents come from God, and when we work on them, we are working side by side with God. When we have completed a task, that in itself is a blessing that should be acknowledged and celebrated. Like any parent who works with their child on a project, God wants to celebrate with us and relish in the completion of the task.

However, at times, we can get too far ahead of ourselves. We forget to enjoy the blessing. Instead, we immediately set a course for the next thing. For example, as James says, we begin to plan where we're going to live next, or how much money we're going to make. All the while forgetting that we are only in this position because of the work we had done with God. It is only through His will that things play out in a way that allows us to do this or that.

Of course we must be wary to never rest on our laurels. I'm only imploring that we take a moment or two longer to acknowledge and enjoy the current blessings we are experiencing; that we don't trivialize them. Yes, one can argue that people have accomplished similar feats, but the point is that *you* accomplished it. There was a time when that task was nothing more than a hope and a goal.

Once we're able to take pleasure in these blessings with God, more blessings will be showered upon us. After allowing myself to bask in the fact that I had finished something I had given my all to, different avenues became clear. My next step solidified. I attacked the task with a newfound vigor and a deeper appreciation of God's will.

The goal is to achieve the dream, whatever that may be for you, but along the way, if we don't learn to appreciate the blessings at hand, then what's the point?

Remember:

1. Delight in your blessings as you become aware of your blessings.

2. But don't become complacent and lose your way. Strike a balance.

3. "Now listen, you who say, 'Today or tomorrow we will go to this or that city, spend a year there, carry on business and make money.' Why, you don't even know what will happen tomorrow. What is your life? You are a mist that appears for a short while and then vanishes. Instead you ought to say, 'If this is the Lord's will, we will live and do this or that.'"
— James 4:13-15

Ramblings on Life – February 18th, 2020 – 5:04AM

It struck me today as I was folding my laundry just how blessed I am. I laughed as I followed this thought. For the last five years, I have been honing my craft by watching some of the greatest films ever made and reading fantastic literature, all while living down the street from the beach. I have spent nights with beautiful and fascinating women. I worked for Apple, down the street from the Santa Monica cliffs that took my breath away upon first sight, and where, hopefully, we'll be shooting the opening of *Meeting Ms. Leigh*. I've driven all over Los Angeles through Lyft and met thousands of interesting people in a very intimate setting. I've shared my dreams and heard stories I'll never forget.

I fell in love with God. I made three short films (two were released). I published four books. I met strangers who became family. I learned to love without needing to be loved back. I was berated by a movie star I once admired over a script *I wrote*. I learned to forgive. I learned patience. I learned it's okay to allow God to break you; He'll always put you back together, and it's

Ramblings on Life – February 18th, 2020 – 5:04AM

ALWAYS for your greatest good. I failed to get my first feature film, *Digits*, off the ground, but that failure gave me *Meeting Ms. Leigh*. I have finally come to understand what they mean by the journey *is* the dream.

Have faith, my friend, I love you.

— R.S. Veira

Definiteness of Purpose

September 21st, 2017

Recently, production wrapped on my newest short film, *The Ride*, and with it concluded a period of time defined by blossoming epiphanies both spiritually and mentally. I wasn't fully aware of the changes these epiphanies brought until the final days of editing the film, but I guess on some level I knew all along that I was undergoing a metamorphosis of sorts.

These changes began around the end of July when I was approached by a woman at work whose story of faith, courage, and success greatly moved me.

Throughout our conversation, she intermittently asked me, "What do you want?" somehow sensing that I was itching to ask questions that I did not know how to articulate. She continued to pry and eventually demanded that I clearly express what I wanted to do and be.

I stated that I was a writer, and I wrote books and scripts. I mentioned that last year I directed a short film that I had also written, more in passing than anything, mainly because it's still in post-production. It was here where my hesitancy lay. Even though I had directed a film, I was not yet ready to call myself a director. The seed had been planted with the production of my first short film, and now this woman had watered it.

I've learned that God will continually offer us opportunities to seize the bountiful future He has in store for us, but we cannot take advantage of these opportunities until we know what we want.

Things moved quickly for me in the weeks following this encounter. On August 1st, I had finished my journey of reading a chapter a day from the Bible, beginning in Genesis and ending in Revelation. It had taken me a few years to do this, and I was now craving further knowledge and understanding, and as these things usually go, I happened to come into possession of two books: *The Law of Attraction* by Esther and Jerry Hicks, and *Think and Grow Rich* by Napoleon Hill. I devoured them both.

After reading these books and beginning the New Testament again, I finally knew very clearly what I wanted to do and what I wanted to be.

I'm a storyteller. I'm an author, a director, and a dreamer. Once this was clear to me and I accepted it as truth, things started to fall into place. In the middle of August, I was approached by a friend, now my new producer and editor, and asked if I had any projects I wanted to work on. I had two ready to go, and I sent him both scripts.

One was *The Ride* and the other was titled *Reflections*. I wanted to do *The Ride* first, mostly because I had tried to get that project off the ground earlier in the year but it never came together, so I had shelved it.

My producer and I met later that week, and we laid out our plan for bringing *The Ride* to life. The following week, we scouted the location and brought on our director of photography. I then reached out to the cast I had used earlier in the year to see if they were interested in giving this another shot; they were.

We began shooting on September 7th and wrapped on the 8th. In those 48 hours, I slept five. I say that to say that for the 43 hours I was awake, I was in perpetual bliss because I was doing what I was born to do. I was telling a story, giving visual life to words I had written, and all within 45 days of my "chance" encounter with that woman at the end of July.

Definiteness of purpose will open more doors than you can ever imagine. All that is required of us is to believe that we can be whatever it is we set out to be, and have the faith that what we envision can be our reality.

To some, this idea is fantastical, and this is because of fear. They are afraid of what they can become. They are afraid of what others will think when they leave the beaten path to chase their dreams. They are afraid of the expectations that come with success and the ***temporary*** sting of failure. But most tragically, they feel that they are undeserving of the dreams they have.

I've been there. As crippling as these fears are, they *can* and *must* be beaten. It begins with earnest belief. It's my deepest yearning and the true purpose of this blog to awaken the dreamer within you. I want nothing more but for that dreamer to realize the dream is possible.

It's as simple as this: If you can see it, believe it, and give everything to it, then you **will** achieve it.

P.S. – *The Ride* will be released on my Vimeo channel next week! To my subscribers, a link will be sent to your email. If you have not yet subscribed, it's never too late!

Remember:

1. Determine what you want to do and who you want to be.

2. Have faith, and you will weather all trials and all obstacles.

3. "Have faith in God," Jesus answered. "I tell you the truth, if anyone says to this mountain 'Go throw yourself into the sea,' and does not doubt in his heart but believes that what he says will happen, it will be done for him. Therefore I tell you, whatever you ask for in prayer, believe that you have received it, and it will be yours."
— Mark 11:22-24

Calm Satisfaction

January 19th, 2018

My third short film, *Reflections*, wrapped last Sunday evening, and afterward, I had no life-changing epiphany, nor was I whisked away by a wave of euphoric glee, but instead I was left with calm satisfaction. It reminded me of one of my favorite Kobe Bryant quotes:

> "When you make a choice and say 'come hell or high water, I am going to be this,' then you should not be surprised when you are that. It should not be something that feels intoxicating or out of character because you have seen this moment for so long that...when that moment comes, of course it's here because it has been here the whole time, because it has been in your mind the whole time."

I had seen *Reflections*' completion long before we began shooting. The production was a personal confirmation that God hears us when we call.

Pre-production for *Reflections* lasted about three months, and as you can imagine, those months were dense with phone calls, emails, and meetings. Every day there was something that had to be done to meet the January 11th shooting date; a date my producer and I had just picked and refused to adjust.

The things that had to be done fell into four major categories: cast, crew, budget, and locations.

The first thing to solidify was the cast. We went through over 400 applications for the various roles and then held auditions for a handful of finalists. From there, we locked in the cast.

The crew, budget, and locations didn't come together until the week before production. During that time, my dependency on God greatly increased, and consequently, our relationship deepened.

The first location we landed was the house of a few friends and former co-workers. They completely opened their doors to us. Which was vitally important, because for us to pull this short film off, we had to be able to manipulate whatever house we got; it was going to be intrusive.

Finding such a house for **free** was an incredible blessing. We secured the next location about six days before shooting. It was a motel two and a half hours outside of Los Angeles. Even though we had to pay for this one, it was more than reasonable.

The assembling of the crew was also quite serendipitous. After meeting with a couple of possible directors of photography, the person who shoots the movie, we couldn't secure one. They were either outside of our budget or other commitments intervened.

We were about two weeks away from filming, and we had no one; so I prayed. I prayed and cried out to God for the crew and budget to materialize in the next 14 days. Things then moved quickly.

A day or two later, I was at In-N-Out and a friend approached me, one whom I hadn't seen in a while, and he informed me that he was a cinematographer. He had seen my last short film, *The Ride*, and wanted to work with me. The timing couldn't have been any better. We locked him in as our director of photography on the 1st of January.

It was also around this time that we received a generous donation to our budget that enabled us to lock in a sound person and makeup artist, both of whom were critical to the production.

We decided that we would need at least $5,000 to make *Reflections*. We were able to raise about $3,000 from the GoFundMe campaign (thank you!) and outside donations. I put up the rest, and just like that, we were ready to shoot on the 11th.

Principal photography began on January 11th. The following four days were a blur where I ate little, slept little, and sustained myself on passion and Red Bull; it was glorious. The cast and crew were focused, efficient, and we worked in harmony to bring my vision to life. I am deeply appreciative of the work they did.

The lesson I pulled from this production was one of steadfastness. I had reached a point in my journey where I challenged myself to no longer doubt God in any capacity. So the moment we decided we were filming from January 11th-14th, I knew that no matter what, we would shoot on those days. I moved forward firmly believing that things would fall into place as they needed to, and they did.

I believe that's how it works. In order to bring these spectacular dreams and ideas we have to life, we have to march toward them with an incredible and irrational faith.

For example, the day before shooting began, we had an accident on set where a U-Haul we rented was sideswiped by a passing driver. We had not purchased the insurance, and the accident set us back a few thousand dollars. In years past, this accident would have given me pause, but this time it made me even more resolute. We were making this movie, and nothing would dissuade me.

If we can only continue to push on with a singular point in mind and believe that the path will reveal itself as we go, it will.

Remember:

1. Set a date for your goal, and move toward it as if there is no doubt in its fruition.

2. Stumbling blocks will arise, but take them in stride. They are only there to test your mettle.

3. "Commit to the Lord whatever you do, and your plans will succeed."

— Proverbs 16:3

Keep Calm & Enjoy the Journey 6
May 3rd, 2018

The purpose of this post is to provide a few updates and to let you know that I'm still chasing my dreams. I hope you are too.

I entered the second quarter of the year (April-June) coming off the high of creation and dealing with the inevitable crash. I had to find a way to settle back into my usual routine after officially wrapping my short film *Reflections*. It was a bumpy transition. My mind went from months of high-octane problem-solving to suddenly having nothing to concentrate on.

For the first few days of April, I took time to reflect (pun intended) on the past seven months, which included the production of my short films *The Ride* and *Reflections*. I took stock of what I had learned and of the things I planned to improve on for my next project. I then laid out my plan for the second and third quarters of the year.

Once the framework for the next six months was set, it was clear to me that it was time to get back in the workshop and again start pounding away at my craft.

I believe discovering our routine and remaining faithful to it is the key to our dreams. For me, that meant two things: getting back into the gym and outlining my main projects for the rest of the year. The gym forces structure and accountability into my days, while outlining is a vital part of my writing process.

It's remarkable how a little bit of structure and focus can cure you of any lethargy. As April wore on, my two new projects for the year took shape. One is a new feature script, and the other is a new e-book.

Finally, I would love to leave you with this nugget.

During one of my recent devotionals, I read the following passage, written by Hannah Whitall Smith, that spoke to my soul:

> *"It is not worthwhile to cry out, 'Oh that I had wings and then I would flee,' for we have the wings already, and what is needed is not more wings, but only that we should use those we have."*

Everything we need to achieve our dreams is within us. God placed these dreams in our hearts so that together, with Him, we could go hand in hand on an awe-inspiring journey to realize them. We are meant to soar with God.

However, in order to do so, we have to first spread our wings; wings that many people do not realize they have. We were not created to simply trudge through misery, pain, and doubt. On the contrary, we were meant to use these stumbling blocks to build our faith and courage so that we can burst triumphantly from the cage of fear that binds so many of us.

In time, through faith in our routine and consistent implementation, our wings are strengthened and we're able to fly as God intended.

So keep pushing and keep dreaming.

Remember:

1. Remaining faithful to our routine is the key to strengthening our wings and achieving our dreams.

2. God wants us to soar with Him.

3. "The dove hath neither claw nor sting,
   Nor weapon for the fight,
   She owes her safety to the wing,
   Her victory to flight.
   The bridegroom opens His arms of love,
   And in them folds the panting dove."

— Hannah Whitall Smith
(*The Christian's Secret of a Happy Life*)

The Matrix of Miracles
August 3rd, 2018

Over the last month, I've been contemplating the nature of miracles and what is necessary for them to occur. It all began after I again read the story of Moses and the Exodus and noticed that God's miracles come to fruition through the mechanics of our reality.

For example, the plague of locusts came on an east wind that blew across the land all day and night (Exodus 10:13). In a similar fashion, the locusts were then taken away by a very strong west wind which carried them to the Red Sea (Exodus 10:19). Finally, when the Red Sea was parted, Moses stretched out his hand over the sea, and all night the Lord drove the sea back with a strong east wind (Exodus 14:21).

Now whether you take these accounts as literal or anecdotal, the lesson is clear. When it comes to miracles, God generally delivers them through agents of our world, and in due time.

Following this train of thought, I began to pore over events I consider miraculous in my own life, and their origins. As I began to trace back events, I quickly realized just how vast and intricate the web of events was and the impeccable timing required for them to occur. It was at that moment it dawned on me why patience is so important.

When we pray and ask God for something and *believe* that He will come through for us, things begin to transpire outside of our knowledge. Miracles are the culmination of innumerable interconnected events. So when we're patient, we allow God to line up the dominoes in such a way that when the first domino falls, it triggers a chain reaction of events that suddenly catapults us to where we've been seeking to be. The transition is so sudden and smooth that to the untrained eye, it's an "overnight success" story. In reality, it was God hearing our pleas and working behind the scenes over a prolonged period of time.

Unfortunately, when we are impatient and force the issue, things tend to fall apart. One of the dominoes that needed a couple more days, weeks, or months to be aligned wasn't given the necessary time, and as a result, things don't come together as smoothly or at all.

I thought about this particular aspect of miracles for a long time because I've been there. I've wanted things so badly that I've reached the point where it's simply inconceivable to wait another moment. But we must. If we can learn this lesson, opportunities beyond our imagination open up to us. I believe we're all here to bring our dreams to fruition, and that only happens through the unity of two or more like minds working in harmony to fulfill the dream at hand.

The creation of such a unity amongst individuals demands that a series of innumerable events unfold on their end and ours. These events lead us to be at the right place at the right time to meet, and also allows for all parties to be in the correct frame of mind so that they're receptive to the dream. When this happens, it's miraculous. When we are impatient with God and trudge forward without Him, we miss these divine appointments.

Now I am not advocating for us to sit around and do nothing. On the contrary, what we must do is what we can do. For example, I'm a writer, and when I focus on my craft and produce content, I ensure that I'm prepared for when one of these appointments occurs. That's how *The Ride* (2017) and *Reflections* (2018) came to be, and it's the reason we're now preparing to attack my first feature-length film, *Digits*.

None of this would've been possible if I had not had scripts ready to go when the opportunity arose. Which, in turn, was only possible because I allowed God to do what God does, while I focused on honing the gift He gave me.

This is not an easy process by any means. It requires a deepening of not only our faith but our dependency on God. This process will subject us to isolation, failure, and at times depression. This is, of course, in addition to the countless outside sources of stress and grief that relentlessly bombard us on a daily basis.

We will question why we do what we do, but if it's what we love and what sprinkles joy into our hearts, then we have to cling to it. And while we're busily clinging to our dream and honing our craft, God is preparing a way.

It's under these conditions that miracles occur. So what skill is God trying to have you hone while He prepares the way for you to step into your dream?

Remember:

1. Be patient, and in the meantime, better your craft.

2. When the moment arrives, be bold and step into your dream.

3. "This is the confidence we have in approaching God: that if we ask anything according to his will, he hears us. And if we know that he hears us—whatever we ask—we know that we have what we asked of him."
   — 1 John 5:14-15

My 4-Year To-Do List (2014-2018)
November 24th, 2018

In 2014, I wrote out a four-year plan. It was really a to-do list made up of things I wanted to accomplish by 2018. At the time, in 2014, I had just graduated from college and was prepping myself for the journey I knew was ahead. I was about to leave for Los Angeles in the summer, and I figured these coming years would be extremely important if I had any hope of honing my craft by the time I reached my thirties. In order to properly navigate these years, I thought it best that I have some milestones set to track my progress.

So, with 2018 coming to a close and those four years on the brink of expiration, it's time to reflect. It was a fascinating exercise. Of the 16 goals I set, I managed to accomplish 10. And when thinking about the 10 I accomplished, none of them happened as I thought they would have. For example, I made a bestseller list, but it was on Amazon and not *The New York Times*.

I also realized, as I was reading the list, that at the time of its creation, I had no other goals besides writing books and short stories. Film was still something I hadn't planned on getting into until later on.

My 4-Year To-Do List (2014–2018)

It's funny how God works.

At the time, I imagined screenwriting was something I would do after my string of successful novels, and who knew when that would be. Directing wasn't even a thought, let alone launching a production company. Yet, at the end of 2018, I've written and directed three short films, I'm in the early stages of pre-production for my first feature-length film (*Digits*), and I have a production company, Dream With Me Productions LLC, with my best friend and business partner, Landen Amos.

Things rarely go as we plan, and that's a good thing. I've learned that it's vitally important for us to take time to envision ourselves years down the line and set milestones, but it's even more crucial that we allow God to work.

I've realized that when we allow God to work and take the lead, He does a very interesting thing. He lets us decide how far we want to go. He places us into situations where we're given the choice to either retreat from Him and fall back in fear of the situation and what it will demand from us OR we can draw closer to Him and expand our dream to encompass the new horizons He has revealed.

I faced such a dilemma when I earnestly began to write and direct films. I was put in a situation where I had to choose to either put off filmmaking for a few more years or seize the opportunity in front of me. I decided to take the opportunity, which immediately meant my dream had to expand, and as it did, so did my need to learn.

Suddenly, I started to meet and foster relationships with individuals who took me under their wing and who fed me films and film literature. They encouraged my curiosity, and soon enough I started seeking ancillary sources of knowledge. Before I knew it, I was immersed in the French New Wave and reading *Hitchcock/Truffaut*.

These four years have taught me that we consistently undersell ourselves and more tragically, God. So as I sit down to write my list for the next four years, I'm going to dream unabashedly and see what situations God puts me in.

I hope you do the same.

P.S. – With the year coming to an end, I've been obsessed with wrapping up a handful of projects that I don't want to bring into the new year unfinished. One of them was the project that served as the impetus for this entire website. I wrote my first novel, *The Last Guardians*, when I was 22 after wrestling with it for two years. Over the last five years, it has been modified and submitted more times than I can count, and I'm finally ready to release it myself. It's coming out next month, and I can't wait to share it with you!

Remember:

1. Dream.

2. Then Dream Bigger.

3. "In order to get to a place called Laity Lodge in Texas, you have to drive into a riverbed. The road takes you down a steep, rocky hill into a canyon and straight into the water. There is a sign at the water's edge which says, 'Yes. You can drive into the water.' One who has made up his mind to go to the uttermost with God will come to a place as unexpected and perhaps looking as impossible to travel as that riverbed looks. He may glance around for an alternative route, but if he wants what God promises His faithful ones, he must go straight into the danger. There is no other way."

— Elisabeth Elliot

Ramblings on Life – November 18th, 2019 – 2:58AM

<u>My Beliefs at 28</u>

1. Pain is purposeful.

2. Love is not possessive.

3. If you ASK, you WILL receive.

4. Anything is possible if you can persevere. Greatness is available for all who choose to have it.

5. There is no rush, everything unfolds at the perfect time if you have faith.

6. Love of the flesh is conditional, only love through the spirit is unconditional.

7. Believe people when they show you who they are, and have compassion.

8. Be cognizant of the blessings that surround you at all times. If you do this, life then becomes a true joy.

9. Love in all circumstances, especially when it's hard.

10. Love yourself.

— R.S. Veira

Managing Disappointment
February 1st, 2019

After suffering a series of disappointments to begin my year, one in particular being that *Reflections* failed to be accepted into any of the film festivals we submitted it to, I was reminded of a lesson I had learned once before. It was one I had forgotten while anticipating *Reflections'* success.

The lesson was that no matter how well we plan or how prepared we think we are for a situation, there are times when things just won't go the way we want them to. These situations can be devastating, and how we handle them reveals just how much we have grown on our journey.

I like to imagine these situations as God testing me to see if I've learned the lesson He's currently been trying to teach me, whatever that may be. So as the doors to various opportunities slammed shut in my face, I remembered this and I wasn't angry, which showed growth, but I was annoyed.

I was annoyed because I had envisioned that *Reflections'* festival success would lead to a bigger opportunity, and that would lead to an even bigger one, and so forth. I was annoyed because I had been praying, studying, and honing my craft, and I just knew that my time was now, but it wasn't. I was annoyed because I allowed myself to get so far ahead of myself.

As I continued to think things over, a fundamental Bible verse came to mind:

> *"And we know that in all things God works for the good of those who love him, who have been called according to his purpose."*
>
> — Romans 8:28

This soothed me, because if we are to believe that there is a master plan at work (and I do), then we have to believe that all events on our journey, good or bad, are meant to prepare us for our ultimate triumph.

This, of course, brought to mind the numerous times in my life when I've been either distraught or lost, and how it wasn't long after these moments of darkness that a great victory came. And with that victory came a deep appreciation for the trials I had faced.

In the midst of trials, disappointments, and failures, I believe it's best to rediscover the joy of our passion. Adversity has a tendency to cloud our vision, and we lose sight of why we're doing all this in the first place.

So for me, I dove into the filmographies of great directors. I've always found solace in studying those who have achieved greatness in whatever I'm pursuing, be it basketball, writing, or directing. There's nothing more inspiring than witnessing someone realize their dream, because that means it's possible; that we all have as good a chance as any to bring our dreams to life.

I took a deep dive into the films of Robert Bresson, Yorgos Lanthimos, Hal Ashby, and Wes Anderson. I'd been meaning to take a deeper look into their work, but until recently hadn't gotten around to it. While I absorbed these directors' stories, the flames of passion that light the depths of my soul were fanned. I knew behind these great works were great trials, but these dreamers had weathered the storm and were ultimately able to share their stories.

I, too, have stories to tell, and I will tell them. Sometimes, we have to be reminded of things like that.

Finally, and most importantly, I had to write. This included outlining new scripts and working on a new *Turner Street* e-book. It also included writing this post. I had to reflect on my failures and come to terms with them. Reconciling with our disappointments and failures is something I believe we have to embrace on this journey.

It's the retooling process after failure and the required reflection that allows us to appreciate the necessity of even the most painful disappointments.

Remember:

1. Take time to examine failure and disappointment. Identify missteps that can be avoided in the future, and take

ownership of the things you could've done better. Next time, you will.

2. Whatever your dream and passion is, don't lose sight of it. But if you do, take the time to rediscover and fall back in love with it. It's a gift from God and one of the most precious things we have. It must be protected.

3. "Every circumstance in life, no matter how crooked and distorted and ugly it appears to be, if it is reacted to in love and forgiveness and obedient to your [God's] will, can be transformed."
— Hannah Hurnard
(*Hinds' Feet on High Places*)

From the Ashes I Rose

June 13th, 2019

It's been a long six months for me, but I finally feel like myself again. I recently finished the rough draft of my second feature-length script, and to say its birth was tumultuous seems to be horribly underselling it.

I'm a firm believer in the idea that God will break us like an egg in order to pour out the creative yoke inside. On our journey to fulfill our dreams and realize our life's purpose, we have to come to trust Him during the pain. In doing so, we learn that in time He'll piece us back together and we'll be all the better for it.

Pain is purposeful. However, when we're in the midst of a storm of doubt and our dinghy is being assaulted by the sea of despair, our understanding that this is purposeful tends to slip our minds.

As I talked about in my last post, the start of my year was full of disappointments and personal failures. During that time, I was emphatically told by a person I once respected, in far more colorful words than this, that:

"You can't write, you'll never make it in this town!"

I was standing on a corner in Santa Monica when this cliché was screamed at me, and it deeply upset me for some time. It was a stain on what was supposed to have been a beautiful day.

We were about to begin the table read for my feature film, *Digits*, (which is just a live reading of a script with actual actors reading the roles) when the movie star in attendance, who had graciously agreed to read with us, made it very clear he didn't like or believe in my material. This devolved into a vicious exchange of words on a street corner in Santa Monica.

That unfortunate situation, coupled with my aforementioned disappointments, sent me spiraling. I soon allowed doubt to take hold, and writing became impossible. The sea of despair pummeled my dinghy, and hope was dying a slow death.

As the storm of doubt intensified, I did the only thing I could do: I prayed. Thankfully, God was quick to answer and reminded me that I've been here before. I was reminded of when I was told I wasn't good enough to play Division I basketball. I remembered the hunger and desire that brought out of me and where God ultimately took me.

So I prayed that I could again use my pain and anger to fuel my dream—that these ordeals would be purposeful. This did not cause the storm to end, but I had found peace in it.

Utilizing this peace, I began to write. My turmoil fueled me, and a new script flowed from me with such ease that I consistently found myself smiling and chuckling as I typed the nights away. Before I knew it, I was over a hundred pages in and the rough draft was complete.

When God breaks us, He does so not to destroy us, but to remodel us into a better version of ourselves. It's a process that requires us to have a deep trust in Him. We have to believe the pain has a purpose, and I can earnestly say it does. To be sitting here with a brand-new script and my creative juices again pumping is a miracle. I'm not only thankful but in awe of God's faithfulness.

So as God finishes piecing me back together and again making me whole, I'm not mad at Him for the painful trials but eternally thankful. They not only made me more resolute in the pursuit of my dream but reminded me to trust Him through the pain. I urge you to do the same. Allow Him to break you and remake you.

Remember:

1. Find peace in the storm.

2. Accept the trial, tribulation, or storm with joy, knowing it's for your betterment.

3. "Therefore I begin to think, my Lord, you purposely allow us to be brought into contact with the bad and evil things that you want changed. Perhaps that is the very reason that we are here in this world, where sin and sorrow and suffering and evil abound, so that we may let you teach us so to react to them, that out of them we can create lovely qualities to live forever."

— Hannah Hurnard
(*Hinds' Feet on High Places*)

Two Sides of the Same Coin

September 20th, 2019

A few days ago, I found myself entrapped by a viscous melancholy, and it was all of my own doing. I was continuously replaying memories and events that served no other purpose but to annoy and frustrate me. I couldn't help myself. I was addicted to the self-pitying feeling of living in pain. If that wasn't bad enough, that particular day was one of the best days I had all year. It was a day full of answered prayers and clever miracles.

Earlier in the day, I found myself at a restaurant in Malibu, pitching my new film (*Meeting Ms. Leigh*) to potential collaborators as the waves of the Pacific Ocean crashed against the beach just outside of the restaurant's French doors. It had been a beautiful day. Yet instead of basking in God's faithfulness, I retreated to the pain of times past and was disgusted with myself.

That disgust, however, turned to intrigue as I began to wonder why it was that when things are going well, we have a tendency to self-sabotage. As I continued to contemplate this, I decided that it boiled down to the two parts of ourselves that are consistently at odds: our flesh and our spirit. But what causes this tension? To answer this, I continued to ponder, and during this period of thorough introspection, I was able to identify the main culprits: unworthiness and fear. After identifying them, I proceeded to defang them, and here is how I did it.

First and foremost, it has to be understood that both the belief of being unworthy and fear are inherent to the flesh. We are beings of both flesh and spirit. Unworthiness and fear do their best to drive a wedge between them, and this can lead to a very contentious inward relationship. Ideally, this relationship should be one of harmony and peace.

It is only through our spirit and the belief in something far grander than ourselves that we can master the flesh and these two saboteurs and achieve inner peace.

The feeling of unworthiness we sometimes get when God smiles on us and answers our prayers is understandable but horribly misguided. In the midst of our blessings, we begin to think whatever is occurring is too good for us and that we don't deserve such grace. This is where we're wrong.

When we think such things, we forget that we are God's children, and like any good parent, God wishes to meet all our needs in abundance. Ideally, children do nothing to earn their parents' love, and parents sacrifice greatly and willingly for their children, just as God did for us with Jesus. Our relationship with God is the idealized version of this dynamic. Understanding this allows us to humble ourselves before God and appreciate our blessings for what they are: acts of love. We could never deserve them, but they're ours nonetheless because God graciously gives them to us.

Humility is inherent to the spirit, and unworthiness withers before it.

Reminding ourselves of this whenever any sense of unworthiness begins to show itself will quickly squash the saboteur. This is similar to how we must handle fear. Fear is tricky in that its arguments can at times be extremely rational and seemingly well thought out. For example, if you're debating on whether to start your own business, fear may declare that doing so would be financially irresponsible. Fear would say:

"We'll not only have to sink all of our money into this venture but most likely other people's, and if we fail, then where would we be? We might as well stay put, it's okay here."

For many of us, this is the end of the conversation, but for us who dare to dream, this is where we must take our stand and our spirit must declare:

"No. It is not okay here. We have something in us, and we must see it through!"

This is faith, and fear will falter here. When the spirit speaks authoritatively to the flesh, the flesh listens because it innately understands that the spirit's authority comes from a much more powerful source. However, fear is persuasive, and if it has been running the show for a while, it will take many of these declarations to subdue it.

Fear deals with what is visible, and to subdue it our spirit must believe without a doubt in what is invisible. Fear's vantage point is finite, and it's scared of what it does not see. To achieve our dreams, we must rely on the one who sees the whole board. So when fear offers its eloquent arguments, our spirit must turn to God and continue forward in faith. The more this is done, the more conviction fear loses until we must strain to hear the once boisterous orator.

There is no defeating unworthiness and fear while we are here on Earth because they are inherent to our flesh. But they can be subdued and mastered through humility and faith, which are inherent to our spirit. When they have been defanged and subdued, our spirit can then look at our flesh with compassion. It's clear that our flesh does not intentionally want to do us harm but does so because it lacks the necessary understanding to do better.

Through faith and humility, our flesh and spirit become one, and we are made whole. When our flesh and spirit walk in tandem, we'll then have the peace necessary to truly enjoy our blessings, and when fear and unworthiness offer up memories of past failures, we'll no longer feel the need to indulge them.

Remember:

1. Mastering the flesh and its companions, fear and unworthiness, is a lifelong process, and knowing that should fill us with even more compassion for ourselves and others.

2. Remember there is a power much grander than ourselves at work, which our spirit draws from. Through humility and faith, fear and unworthiness are subdued.

3. "So I say, live by the Spirit, and you will not gratify the desires of the flesh. For the flesh desires what is contrary to the Spirit, and the Spirit what is contrary to the flesh. They are in conflict with each other, so that you do not do what you want."

— Galatians 5:16-17

Ramblings on Love – August 17th, 2019 – 4:50AM

I want to have a family like my parents. I want my family to laugh long and hard and rejoice in the blessings of God. I want us to pull for one another and be there for one another. I want us to love unconditionally and fiercely. I want to raise such a family with the woman that God has chosen for me, and I her. I pray that we lay down our egos and pride for one another, that we give God our relationship, and that by doing so we decide to always regard each other with compassion. I pray both of us understand that even though we will at times hurt one another and succumb to our human foibles, we will never abandon each other. I pray that our home is full of love, and by that, I can only mean God. Amen.

Have faith, my friend, I love you.

— R.S. Veira

A Decade of Highs & Sighs

December 30th, 2019

Over the last month, I've been taking stock of the last 10 years, and it's been one hell of a decade. Ten years ago this month, I had just transferred high schools. I left a school I had attended since kindergarten in order to chase a dream. I left friends and close relationships I'd fostered over the entirety of my scholastic career in hopes of achieving that dream. That decision set the tone for my decade, and I don't think it's hyperbolic to say it set the tone for the rest of my life.

In 2014, I fulfilled that dream and graduated from Cleveland State University after playing Division I basketball for two and a half years. From there, my focus shifted fully to my next dream, and I began writing in earnest. The next five years were deeply humbling and trying. I published the *Turner Street Chronicles* and *The Last Guardians*. I wrote and directed three short films (two were released) and then tried to make my first feature film, *Digits*.

I was unsuccessful in getting *Digits* off the ground, but that failure begat an even better opportunity. With the decade closing, I'm again gearing up for my first feature film, this time it's

Meeting Ms. Leigh. It's an entirely new project that's only possible because of the failure of my first. This is a perfect example of one of the most important things I've learned this decade: that God will send us on test runs to prepare us for the real race.

It's a simple enough idea, but the problem is that we sometimes mistake the test run for the main event. We become so dejected and resentful when we fail because we don't believe another opportunity is coming. We don't trust God, who was the author of the initial opportunity in the first place.

If we truly believe that God is the author of all things, that He has plans for us to prosper, and that everything works for our good, then we can rest assured that that opportunity will not be the last. No matter how many times we fail, as long as we push forward in faith, new opportunities will arise.

The purpose of these test runs is to show us where we're lacking so that our weaknesses and shortcomings can be addressed. The obstacles in our way are not meant to destroy our confidence but to ultimately build it. So when it's time to run the real race, we'll not only be fleet of foot but run without growing weary.

In the latter half of this decade, I've realized that from a high enough vantage point, every failure, disappointment, and moment of pain can be seen ultimately as good. If used properly, they'll humble us and force us to reassess our trajectory. They'll push us closer to God, and in doing so we'll become more comfortable in asking Him for directions.

When my first attempt to make a feature film failed, I was initially distraught. I thought that was my opportunity; that a better one might not come. Looking back, I now see that I wasn't yet ready for the task in the first place. I now realize God needed me to not only continue to hone my craft but to experience things that would inspire me to write something I'd be willing to go the distance to make. Something truly near and dear to my heart.

I had to be humbled and broken this decade so that God could give me what I prayed for.

With a new decade on the horizon, I find myself gleeful. I don't know where God will lead me over the next 10 years, but I know it'll be a fulfilling and worthwhile journey. It will undoubtedly be trying at times, but thankfully, God has spent this decade showing me what He can do if I can only remain persistent and hopeful.

Finally, and most importantly, God allowed me to write all these things down and share them with you so that you, too, will stay the course and not lose heart.

Remember:

1. Never stop. Everything comes together in due time.

2. "I love the Lord, for he heard my voice; he heard my cry for mercy. Because he turned his ear to me, I will call on him as long as I live."
   — Psalm 116:1-2

3. "Because he loves me," says the Lord, "I will rescue him; I will protect him, for he acknowledges my name. He will call upon me and I will answer him; I will be with him in

trouble, I will deliver him and honor him. With long life I will satisfy him and show him my salvation."

— Psalm 91:14-16

Why Do We Do What We Do?

March 13th, 2020

It's taken me a long time to sit down and write this post. Over the last month or so, I've been trying to figure out exactly what I wanted to say, and this is the product of my musing.

On January 26th, 2020, God took home my childhood hero, Kobe Bean Bryant, and a week later, on February 2nd, 2020, God welcomed home my cousin Zachery Eldemire. I will miss them both dearly.

Kobe was 41 and Zach was 26. Both of their lives were heading in exciting new directions, and yet already knowing this, God chose these dates for them long before their first breath. God's timing is perfect; He is good and does not make mistakes. God is love. So with all that in mind, I began to contemplate the ultimate purpose for our time here on Earth.

Over the years, I have come to realize it's true that those who ask receive, and those who seek find. So it was no surprise when everything in my life seemed to line up in accordance with my current pursuit for answers. When these tragedies struck, I just so happened to reach Ecclesiastes during my daily devotional, which is a book in the Bible where King Solomon ponders and pursues the meaning behind our toils on Earth. Concurrently, I was reading *The Bridge of San Luis Rey* and *The Master and Margarita*.

The Bridge of San Luis Rey, written by Thornton Wilder, is about five travelers who fall to their deaths when the eponymous bridge collapses. The novel tells the story of each of these travelers and how they ended up on the bridge on that fateful day. *The Master and Margarita*, written by Mikhail Bulgakov, is a novel about the devil coming to Moscow and the effects his arrival has on all its inhabitants, especially The Master and his lover, Margarita.

Ecclesiastes, *The Bridge of San Luis Rey*, and *The Master and Margarita* all center on the absurdity of our existence and the various ways we all decide to spend it. Ecclesiastes puts forth a thorough and passionate case that all our pursuits in life are ultimately meaningless and steeped in vanity. Solomon concludes that all a man (or woman) can hope to do is fear God, keep His commandments, and find satisfaction in his/her toiling on Earth. He states that this is in fact a gift from God, because if we learn to do these things, then our days will be filled with peace, joy, and love in spite of our circumstances.

The Bridge of San Luis Rey paints a poignant picture of how death comes unexpectedly for us all no matter how prosperous or destitute we may be. *The Master and Margarita* is in itself an illustration of how little control we have over our own narrative or how we will be remembered. Mikhail Bulgakov's masterpiece was published decades *after* his death and is considered not only his finest work but one of the great works of literature. Bulgakov never enjoyed the fruits of his labor, yet his work has inspired and touched the hearts of millions.

Death has a way of distilling the vital things from life. All we *truly* have are our God-given dreams. So we must have the courage to acknowledge these dreams and pursue them. This will send us on a life-defining journey that demands a deep communion with God. It's on this journey that we truly meet Him and fall in love. This is the journey to a fully realized life.

For this reason, we must be resolute in the pursuit of our dreams. The pursuit is our purpose. What's truly important is who we become on the journey to our dream's fulfillment, not the accolades and wealth we hope to get when we arrive. We may never eat the fruit of our labor the way we imagined, but we can take solace in the fact that whatever we create and leave behind has a chance to inspire and bring joy to those who come after us.

On our journey with God to fulfill our dreams, we'll eventually realize that the journey is what it's all about. Through the journey, we learn how to move out of love and not fear, how to love deeply and unabashedly, and how to pour ourselves out for those in need.

When our heroes or loved ones pass unexpectedly, we're not only devastated but plagued by confusion and blinded by grief. However, in time, from the cataclysm blooms a rose of hope. We are hopeful for our future reunion, and this hope eventually begets joy. We are joyful and thankful that God allowed us to love and experience these individuals and for the marks they left on our lives. Their deaths inspire us to live better.

I believe that is our ultimate purpose, to live such a full and rich life that our passing inspires others to dream bigger, to love deeper, and to be better. A life like that can only be attained through the pursuit of our dreams.

Rest in peace, Zach and Kobe, my prayers and condolences go out to everyone who has lost someone this year. May we honor their memory with fully realized lives.

Remember:

1. The death of those we love and care for deeply is undeniably painful, but like all pain, it is purposeful.

2. Use your time wisely and ardently; you never have as much as you think.

3. "I know there is nothing better for men than to be happy and do good while they live. That everyone may eat and drink, and find satisfaction in all his toil— this is the gift of God."
   — Ecclesiastes 3:12-13

The Shattering of My Fetters

November 2nd, 2020

I shaved my head last week, and by doing so the last fetters of insecurity that had prevented my soul from soaring as it was meant to were shattered.

For the last few years, the anxiety over my receding hairline had grown to the point where it had become a barrier between God and me. As vain as it sounds, I was annoyed that God was taking my hair. It goes to show that even the smallest things can be barriers between God and us. However, God responded to my insolence with an abundance of grace and love.

For the last few years, I've felt like I've been wandering about in a spiritual wilderness of sorts. It was a time when God was separating me from the things I had been chasing to give me the fulfillment that I now know is impossible outside of God. It was a time marked by isolation, contemplation, and deeply humbling experiences.

I've talked about a majority of these events to various extents, but it wasn't until I was reading Patrick Morley's *How God Makes Men: Ten Epic Stories. Ten Proven Principles. One*

Huge Promise For Your Life that I saw how God had orchestrated all these events to ultimately free me from my spiritual fetters.

There comes a point on our journey to fulfill our dreams that God has to take us aside and fix our character, or whatever He eventually blesses us with will ultimately ruin us because we are apt to worship the blessing over the one who blessed us.

However, in order for God to refine our character we have to trust Him and surrender our will to Him, and in order for us to do that *willingly*, we have to believe that God is indeed love and that he loves us beyond any reasonable comprehension.

During my time in the wilderness, God proved that to me. He painstakingly showed me through a series of events and various people in my life that He is in fact love and can be trusted without a shadow of a doubt.

This culminated in the arrival of Mr. Morley's book, which I received during a prayer walk earlier this year in downtown Los Angeles following George Floyd's murder. I quickly devoured it, and I immediately felt God moving my soul to share the book with some of the men in my life. Since I had been walking with God so intimately over the last few years, I recognized His gentle whispering voice and did not dismiss it as we are prone to do when we do not know Him well.

The wilderness had taught me many of God's promises, and one of them is that if you ask, you shall receive, so I prayed for clarity and help. I had never facilitated a small group like the one

I was proposing, and I didn't know how to go about it. Thankfully, as promised, the help and clarity I had requested was graciously given to me. Within a few days, I had a list of men I wanted to reach out to, and my (earthly) father, a deacon, sent me a few books that helped prepare me for the task at hand.

Over the next 10 weeks, I met weekly with about 10 other men. They were split up into two groups that met on Friday nights and Sunday mornings, respectively. Together, we went on a journey to better understand God and what it means to be His child. It was a truly beautiful experience, and at the conclusion of the 10 weeks, we began a Bible study that is still ongoing.

This act of faithfulness on God's part encouraged me to at last bring to Him my remaining great insecurity, my hair. I prayed for guidance and for Him to be with me when I shaved it.

I set a date, and when the day came, I welcomed it with excitement and a surprisingly peaceful soul. For another one of God's promises is that if there is anything at all that makes us anxious, we are to quickly bring it to Him and leave it with Him. He will then graciously take on our burdens and give our souls rest.

So with my soul at peace, I picked up my clippers and began. As my hair fell to the ground, my grin grew more and more, because to my amazement, I loved it. I loved my now gleaming dome.

I realized then and there that if we can only gather the courage to dive into our fears, worries, and insecurities, we'll find that God is right there in the midst of it all, waiting to lovingly show us that there is in fact nothing to fear. On the other side of our so-called brokenness and insecurities, which were mostly forced upon us by a world that does not know God, is actually what makes us unimaginably beautiful.

During this time, I was also reading Hannah Whitall Smith's masterpiece *The Christian's Secret of a Happy Life*. I cannot recommend this book enough. Mrs. Smith logically explains that in order for our souls to fly as they were meant to, they must use their wings, which she named Surrender and Trust. We must surrender our will to God and trust that His promises are true.

His promises are many, and they are all fabulous and we must trust them. If we can do this, then there is no obstacle on this earth that can deter us nor prison that can contain us, and we will soar to the highest heights.

For example, it is through this flight of the soul that Nelson Mandela was able to serve over two decades of an unjust prison sentence and come out a shining emblem of love and righteousness. It is by the same flight of the soul that Joseph was able to endure both slavery and imprisonment without allowing them to harden his heart.

When God graciously granted Joseph great stature in Egypt, he did not shame his brothers who sold him into slavery but was able to forgive them and lovingly embrace them. It is by this *same* flight of the soul that we are able to overcome any situation or obstacle that may come against us while we endeavor to achieve our dreams.

However, we will never fly if we do not face the insecurities and brokenness that we hide in the darkest corners of our souls and that we allow to weigh us down.

No matter how small we may think they are, they are enough to hinder our ability to fly. The only way to free ourselves is to surrender them to God and to trust that He will give us peace, and He will. Believe me, my friends, He will.

My friends and fellow dreamers, I entreat you to surrender, to trust, and to fly. Do not subscribe to the ideas of the world that say you are not enough, or that you are unfit. Do not let the world cage you in. You are a child of the Most High God, who created you to soar with Him, not just in the hereafter, but in the here and now.

Spread your wings and set yourself free.

Remember:

1. You are a child of God, and your soul was made to fly.

2. God does not subject us to unnecessary obstacles. Everything is meant to facilitate our soul's freedom. Trust that He loves you, and surrender to His loving will.

3. "No earthly bars can ever imprison the soul. No walls however high, or bolts however strong, can imprison an eagle so long as there is an open way upward; and earth's power can never hold the soul in prison while the upward way is kept open and free. Our enemies may build walls around us as high as they please, but they cannot build any barrier between us and God; and if we 'mount up with

wings' we can fly higher than any of their walls can ever reach."

—Hannah Whitall Smith

4. "But those who hope in the Lord shall renew their strength. They will soar on wings like eagles; they will run and not grow weary, they will walk and not be faint."

— Isaiah 40:31

Ramblings on God – February 23rd, 2021 – 2:14AM

Keep Calm & Enjoy the Journey VII

I think my journey with my blog in its present form has come to an end. I think I've said all I need to say at this point, and I'm ready to compile everything from the last five years or so. A series of new opportunities has suddenly arisen, and I'm excited to see what will come of them.

I was telling Landen a few days ago, after all that's happened out here, there is no longer any sensible reason to doubt. God has been faithful. The spiritual foundation of Dream With Me Productions has been laid. We now must build on top of it efficiently and purposefully. We must use the lumber of Love, the nails and bolts of Grace, and the tools of Faith to build the most glorious spiritual edifice imaginable so that Dream With Me Productions' soul is right.

Then, God willing, it may be a place where great work is done out of love and not out of selfish ambition, pride, or greed. A place where bold and courageous dreamers gather to do great work and pay no mind to fear. A place where we believe without constraint for we know, without a doubt, that God is real.

God has shown me that prayer can move mountains and that believers united in prayer can move the cosmos. When we pray, God will at times give us glimpses of Him working on whatever it is we've prayed for. These glimpses can be a phone call, or a conversation with a friend, or anything that God chooses, really, but the point is to reveal a bit of information previously unknown to us that shows He's moving things in our favor. It's at this point that we must be even more persistent in our prayers because now we have confirmation that God heard us. We must hold on to the hope that these glimpses provide and double down on our belief that God will fulfill what we have asked of Him.

If my blog has shown me anything, it's that He is faithful and really is capable of doing immeasurably more than all we can ask or imagine according to HIS power at work within us. Prayer builds faith, and by building our faith, we allow for more of His power to pulsate through us and our lives. We then open the door to miracles that are so sublime that words cannot describe. Wonders that our souls have always yearned for but were unable to articulate or too afraid to ask for.

So let us now be steady and resolute in our prayers and dreams. Let us wait expectantly for what God has in store for us and enjoy the journey He has lovingly laid out for us. It's a glorious blessing to be alive and chasing a dream. Let's take full advantage of it.

My friend, have faith, be patient, never settle, and dream. I love you.

— R.S. Veira

Submission

(A Poem)

He who knows where the wind goes and where darkness resides,
He who knows why light shines and birds fly,
He who cradles my soul and smiles from on high
Says to me, "Young King, I love you, do you now see?"
I smile and reply, "My Beloved, I do, and I'll do whatever you please."
He laughs and extends a hand, "Then let us go, there is much to see."
In His grasp, I whisper, "As you wish, and thank you for saving me."

— R.S. Veira

(6-19-20 5:43pm)

About the Author

R.S. Veira is an author, director, and dreamer. He is currently writing, directing, and dreaming at Dream With Me Productions in Los Angeles, California. To learn more about R.S. Veira and his writing, visit him at rsveira.com.

www.ingramcontent.com/pod-product-compliance
Lightning Source LLC
Chambersburg PA
CBHW030902080526
44589CB00010B/114